The Gospel
of John

The Gospel of John

An Exposition by
Charles R. Erdman

BAKER BOOK HOUSE
Grand Rapids, Michigan 49506

Paperback edition reprinted by Baker Book House with permission of The Westminster Press

ISBN: 0-8010-3400-0

First printing, November 1983
Second printing, December 1984

Printed in the United States of America

PREFACE

Atheism was not a problem for the writers of either the Old or the New Testaments. They spent neither space nor energy to prove the existence of God. They simply told about the mighty acts of God; about his sole sovereignty; and of his purpose to make his salvation available to all who would obey and trust him. Through a chosen people God would become known if they were faithful, and in the fullness of time he would send forth his Son, born of a woman, born under the law, to bring redemption.

The New Testament writers all believed that Jesus of Nazareth was the Son of God, fully God and fully man. Nothing like this had ever occurred previously in human history, and it would never occur again. In this Jesus, God revealed himself fully. Men no longer needed to inquire, "What is God like?" They could see Jesus and know that whoever had seen him with the eyes of faith has seen God.

The Gospel of John has probably been among the greatest influences in history to turn men from sin to righteousness. It begins by explaining that Jesus was God as the Word (*Logos*). All things were made through him. In him was life. He came into our world to bring the life abundant to all who would believe in him, to whom he gave power to become the children of God. As page after page of the Gospel unfolds we may read of the many ways in which testimony to Jesus' Sonship was certified, not only by human witnesses but also by the *signs* through which he manifested his gift of abundant and eternal life.

Bible-reading and study are effective means of inducing men, women, and children to get a God's-eye image of themselves. This may lead them to pray that their marred image be restored through the forgiving love of God in Christ Jesus. It is well-nigh impossible to read what

Jesus said to Nicodemus, who came by night, without hearing the still, small voice of the Gospel whisper in one's soul, "You must be born anew." One cannot easily evade the logic of ch. 7:17, "If any man's will is to do his will, he shall know whether the teaching is from God." And who can doubt the love of God after meditating on ch. 3:16!

But it is not the purpose of a preface to do the task of the expositor. Dr. Charles R. Erdman, the expositor for each of the seventeen volumes in this New Testament series, has done a magnificent explanation and interpretation of John's Gospel. A glance through his introduction should whet the appetite to sit under his tutelage until this Gospel has been thoroughly digested. His outline of the Gospel provides a preview and analysis of the entire content and message. Following each printed section of the Gospel text, Dr. Erdman explains the Gospel author's meaning, and often suggests how the message is applicable to contemporary situations.

Pastors have found Dr. Erdman's insights not only an opening of the Scripture but also a seedbed from which sermons sprout. Church school teachers lean heavily on this series as they prepare to meet their classes; they recommend the volumes to their students. College and seminary professors make the volumes available in libraries.

The constant demand for the Erdman commentaries has badly worn the type and plates. This new paperback edition is printed from a completely new set.

EARL F. ZEIGLER

FOREWORD

The guiding principle in these expository studies has been to trace, through the successive scenes of the Gospel, the definite purpose of its author, and to note the witness he has borne to the divine Person of our Lord, to the development of faith and unbelief, and especially to the life in which faith issues. It is one of many approaches to this inspired masterpiece, but it cannot fail to bring us near to the heart of its message. Limitations of space have made it necessary to exclude all illustrations and quotations from related literature, and to depend, for sustained interest, upon the fascination of the narrative, and the supreme importance of the truths it presents.

INTRODUCTION

The Fourth Gospel is the most familiar and the best-loved book in the Bible. It is probably the most important document in all the literature of the world. It has induced more persons to follow Christ, it has inspired more believers to loyal service, it has presented to scholars more difficult problems, than any other book that could be named.

The peculiar character of the book has been set forth by the single adjective "sublime"; for sublimity is said to result from the two factors of simplicity and profundity. The sea is sublime, because of its unbroken expanse and its measureless depths; and the cloudless sky is sublime because of its limitless vaults of blue. Such, too, is this little book; its stories are so simple that even a child will love them, but its statements are so profound that no philosopher can fathom them.

The author, almost beyond question, was John, who was among the first followers of Christ, belonged to the inner circle of the apostles, stood at the cross, received to his home the mother of our Lord, was the first to believe his resurrection, and lingered last, looking for his Master's return. He never names himself in the narrative, but assumes the title of "the disciple whom Jesus loved," suggesting how the love of Christ inspired and transfigured him. Surely such a person was best prepared to write of the nature and life of Christ. For centuries the symbol of the Gospel has been the "eagle," the bird which is said to soar highest and to gaze with unveiled eye upon the dazzling brightness of the sun.

The purpose of the author is indicated in the opening eighteen verses, commonly called the Prologue, and is definitely stated in the closing sentences of the twentieth chapter: "That ye may believe that Jesus is the Christ, the Son of God; and that believing ye may have life in his name." He wishes, therefore, to prove that Jesus is the "Messiah" who came in fulfillment of all the Old Testament types and prophecies; and further that he is a divine Being and is in this unique sense "the Son of God." The ultimate purpose, however, is to inspire in his readers such faith in Christ as will result in that eternal life which Christ alone can give. In order to effect his purpose, John produces a number of witnesses, which have been variously classified, and include the testimony of the Father, of the Holy Spirit, of the Scriptures, of John the Baptist, of the disciples, of various individuals, such as Nicodemus, the woman of Samaria, Pilate, Caiaphas; but above all, John depends upon the testimony of the words and works of Jesus. If he was not "the Christ, the Son of God," then his claims were those of a deceiver; if he did not work miracles, he surely pretended to, and was then an imposter. Of these miracles John makes a careful selection of only seven or eight; and it is in reference to these "signs" of divine power that John declares, "these are written, that ye may believe."

The method of John in presenting his proof is not that of a logical treatise or philosophical argument; he has rather presented a drama. The life of Christ, which is the substance of his Gospel, is written with the fascination of a play; but as each actor steps upon the scene some new testimony is borne to the fact that Jesus is the Christ, the Son of God; and as the testimony is produced, and as Christ makes his claims and works his miracles, we see the developing faith of his followers and the deepening hatred of his enemies.

There are two great parts to the dramatic action. The first closes with the twelfth chapter. The last great miracle has been wrought; Lazarus has been raised from the dead, and now the rulers conspire to put Jesus to death; but Mary appears pouring out upon the feet of her Lord her priceless gift of love, and the multitudes greet him with hosannas, and even the Greeks are eager to see him. In the second part of the book, Christ has withdrawn from the world and is revealing himself to his disciples, first in an act of humble service, then in words of comfort and cheer, then in a prayer which none but the Son of God could have uttered, and supremely in his triumph over pain and suffering and death. When at last the doubting Thomas stands before his risen Master, and cries out, "My Lord and my God," the demonstration is complete; there is no reason why all readers should not believe that Jesus is the Christ, the Son of God.

Yet, the purpose of John is intensely practical; he wishes not only to inspire faith but to show the life in which faith will issue. This is the significance of the miracles which he relates; they are indeed "signs" of divine power, but they are also symbols of the life which Christ imparts. The first was wrought in a home at a wedding feast, to suggest the joy of the Christian life and the transforming power of Christ. The second shows how Christ can deliver from fear and anxiety, as he restores hope and peace to a parent's heart. Then he heals a cripple, to indicate his ability to give power to the helpless. He feeds the five thousand to reveal himself as the real Food for the soul. He stills the storm, and men learn what he can be to them in all times of stress and places of peril. He opens the eyes of one born blind and teaches us that he alone can take away "the dimness of our souls." He raises Lazarus, and we understand his claim to be "the resurrection, and the life." He rises victorious over death and the grave, and we no longer doubt that he is divine, but cry out adoringly, "Our Lord and our God."

It only remained for John to write that charming Epilogue which forms the last chapter of his Gospel, where we see that a divine Lord is also an unseen, present, guiding, sustaining Lord; and where we find that faith will issue in lives of service and love and patient suffering, as we wait for our Lord to reappear in visible glory.

THE OUTLINE

I

THE PROLOGUE   *John 1:1-18*   13

II

THE REVELATION TO THE WORLD, AND THE
DEVELOPMENT OF FAITH AND UNBELIEF
                        Chs. 1:19 to 12:50   19

A. The Preparation   *Chs. 1:19 to 2:11*   19
   1. The Witness of the Forerunner   *Ch. 1:19-34*   19
   2. The Witness of the First Followers
                        Ch. 1:35-51   23
   3. The Witness of the First Miracle   *Ch. 2:1-11*   27
B. The Public Ministry   *Chs. 2:12 to 12:50*   31
   1. The Opening of the Ministry   *Chs. 2:12 to 4:54*   31
      a. The Witness in Jerusalem
                        Chs. 2:12 to 3:21   31
      b. The Witness in Judea   *Ch. 3:22-36*   41
      c. The Witness in Samaria   *Ch. 4:1-42*   43
      d. The Witness in Galilee   *Ch. 4:43-54*   50
   2. The Fuller Manifestation   *Chs. 5 to 11*   53
      a. The "Sign" on the Sabbath; and the
         Beginning of the Conflict   *Chs. 5 to 8*   53
      b. The Sixth "Sign"; and the Formal Breach
         with the Religious Leaders   *Chs. 9; 10*   86
      c. The Supreme "Sign"; and the Conspiracy
         of the Rulers   *Ch. 11*   101
   3. The Close of the Ministry   *Ch. 12*   112
      a. The Manifestations of Faith   *Ch. 12:1-36*   113
      b. The Condemnation of Unbelief
                        Ch. 12:37-50   121

III

THE REVELATION TO THE DISCIPLES, AND THE
CULMINATION OF FAITH AND UNBELIEF
Chs. 13 to 20   124

A. The Private Teaching *Chs. 13 to 17*   124
   1. The Ministry of Love *Ch. 13*   124
   2. The Words of Cheer *Chs. 14 to 16*   131
   3. Jesus' Intercessory Prayer *Ch. 17:1-26*   150
B. The Supreme Witness *Chs. 18 to 20*   157
   1. The Betrayal and Trial *Chs. 18:1 to 19:16* 157
   2. The Crucifixion *Ch. 19:17-42*   168
   3. The Resurrection *Ch. 20*   175

IV

THE EPILOGUE. THE PRESENCE AND THE SYMBOLIC
"SIGN" *Ch. 21*   182

I
THE PROLOGUE
John 1:1-18

How shall we regard Jesus Christ? Is he to be admired as the best of men, or may he also be worshiped and trusted as God; was he the greatest of prophets, or is he also the Messiah, the predicted Savior of the world?

Then, again, does it really matter how we regard him? Is it true that our attitude toward him is a test of character, and that belief in him affects life and determines destiny?

Then further, has there been given us sufficient evidence on which to base our belief, and do we have such testimony as to warrant our trust?

With these three great questions the Gospel of John is continually concerned; and they find definite answers in the first eighteen verses, which form a preface, or introduction, and are commonly called the Prologue.

Here it is affirmed that Jesus Christ has ever existed as God, as, indeed, the Creator by whom all things were made. It is also stated that faith in him results in such a moral transformation as can best be described as being "born of God." It is further indicated that this faith is based on the witness of men who were his intimate companions, in the days of his flesh, and who spoke from personal experience.

Thus the Prologue presents all the essential ideas of the Gospel, as it deals with the testimony to the Person of Christ, the manifestation of faith and unbelief, and the issue of faith in life. (John 20:30-31.)

These verses have been variously analyzed. It may be helpful to divide them into three short paragraphs, and to notice that, while all embody the great ideas of the Gospel, each emphasizes a particular truth which may be indicated as follows: Verses 1-5, Christ the Revealer of God; verses 6-13, the response of unbelief and faith; verses 14-18, the experience of believers.

In all three paragraphs the thought moves through the same spheres, but it advances from the more remote to the nearer in time, from the more general to the more specific, from the abstract to the concrete and personal; but it is always concerned with Christ, and it reaches its climax in the statement of the last verse relative to his divine Person and mission.

> *1 In the beginning was the Word, and the Word was with God, and the Word was God. 2 The same was in the beginning with God. 3 All things were made through him; and without him was not anything made that hath been made. 4 In him was life; and the life was the light of men. 5 And the light shineth in the darkness; and the darkness apprehended it not.*

Verses 1-5. It would be difficult to imagine a more profound statement as to the Person of Christ. He is here set forth in his relation to God and the world, and specifically as the self-revelation of God. The statements are timeless and universal, and are not to be limited to the activity of the preincarnate Christ. He has always been revealing God, both in creation and in the moral consciousness of men; but men have always been slow to apprehend him, or unwilling to accept him.

He is introduced as "the Word," a term which might mean "the reason," either as it exists in the mind or is outwardly expressed in speech. Both meanings are true of Christ as "the Word" of God. He is one with the very being and mind of God; he is also the expression of the intelligence and will and power of God. His Person is identified with God; his office is to reveal God. Thus in the first two verses it is declared that he has existed from "the beginning," that he was in a personal relation to God, and that he was one in essence with God; so that in a single sentence the eternity, personality, and deity of Christ are all affirmed.

In the third and fourth verses he is described as revealing God, in the creation of the world, and in continuing to be the source of all life. For men, in whom life developed in the form of rational and moral being, he is also "the light," or the Source of all truth.

The fifth verse declares that while, in reason and conscience and in the Person of Christ, this divine Light of truth has ever been shining, it has ever been obscured by the moral and spiritual darkness of the world; men have never been able to understand Christ, nor have they been willing to submit to him. Thus in its opening paragraph the tragedy of this Gospel is introduced. Yet, while the rejection of Christ is to be recorded, some are to accept him and to find through him true life and light. This manifestation of unbelief and faith forms the substance of the next section.

6 There came a man, sent from God, whose name was John. 7 The same came for witness, that he might bear witness of the light, that all might believe through him. 8 He was not the light, but came *that he might bear witness of the light. 9 There was the true light, even the light which lighteth every man, coming into the world. 10 He was in the world, and the world was made through him, and the world knew him not. 11 He came unto his own, and they that were his own received him not. 12 But as many as received him, to them gave he the right to become children of God, even to them that believe on his name: 13 who were born, not of blood, nor of the will of the flesh, nor of the will of man, but of God.*

Verses 6-13. As the writer here proceeds to state the great historic failure of the world to receive Christ, he first mentions the ministry of John the Baptist, whose work seemed calculated to make such a failure impossible, whose testimony made it appear more pitiful and perverse.

John is called "a man," and the preceding statements as to the deity of Christ are at once emphasized by the contrast; so, too, he was "sent from God," he was not God. Nor yet was he "the light"; but he was a great "witness," and by the emphatic statement of verses seven and eight we are introduced to a feature of the Gospel which must ever be kept in mind. This Gospel is a record of testimony and shows that faith is belief founded upon evidence.

The testimony is to Christ, of whom it is stated, in verse nine, that by his "coming into the world" he has become "the true light" for every man who will receive him.

The verse does not mean to identify Christ with the universal conscience, nor to assert, however true it may be, that there is moral light in every man. The phrase, "coming into the world," refers to Christ, and not to "every man." He is "the true light" for everyone who accepts him; but the world, as a whole, has been too blind or too wicked to welcome him, as is asserted in verse ten. The next verse tells us that when he came to the place and the people especially prepared for his coming, he was not received.

In this reference to the relation of Christ to the Jewish nation, "he came unto his own," there is another touch characteristic of John. He is here intimating that Christ was the Messiah of the Jews, and to establish this fact was one of the great purposes of his Gospel.

"He came unto his own [things], and . . . his own [people] received him not." However, there were those who were ready to receive him. This Gospel is not only a tragedy of unbelief, it is also a great drama of the unfolding of faith; and the writer now suggests another characteristic feature of his Gospel as he shows how faith issues in life. This life is that of true "children of God." "As many as received him, to them gave he the right [or privilege] to become children of God." The term "children," used by John, is distinct from the term "sons" which is more commonly used by Paul. Both terms apply to all Christians, but the latter suggests position and legal rights secured by adoption; the former indicates likeness, nature, life, resulting from birth. This "new birth" of believers is declared to be "not of blood," i.e., by heredity or inheritance, "nor of the will of the flesh," i.e., by natural instinct, "nor of the will of man," i.e., by human volition, "but of God," i.e., by the direct, supernatural exercise of divine power. Therefore, the life of a true Christian cannot be explained on the grounds of heredity, or of environment, or of personal resolution; it is imparted by the Spirit of God.

14 And the Word became flesh, and dwelt among us (and we beheld his glory, glory as of the only begotten from the Father), full of grace and truth. 15 John beareth witness of him, and crieth, saying, This was he of whom I said, He that cometh after me is become before me: for he was before me. 16 For of his fulness we all received, and grace for grace. 17 For the law was given through Moses; grace and truth came through Jesus Christ. 18 No man hath seen God at any time; the only begotten Son, who is in the bosom of the Father, he hath declared him.

Verses 14-18. John now states that the appearance of "the Word," the shining of "the true light," the "coming into the world," was by way of incarnation: "the Word became flesh." The term "flesh" denotes human nature, but not, as usually in the writings of Paul, sinful nature. When "the Word became flesh" he did not cease to be what he had been, but as an additional experience he assumed human nature. He became the God-Man, at the same time "perfect God and perfect man," an absolutely unique being. As, of old, God dwelt in a tabernacle in the midst of Israel, so, we read, he "dwelt [tabernacled] among us," in the Person of Christ. "We beheld his glory, glory as of the only begotten from the Father, full of grace and truth," i.e., his glory was a manifestation of the spiritual splendor, of the divine love and holiness of God; but he was "the only begotten," absolutely distinct from those who are called the "children of God" by faith in him. In the last clause of the Prologue the term "only begotten" is again repeated, and here the true reading, according to the best Greek text, seems to be "the only begotten God."

Such is the conception which the writer has of the Person of Christ, and in this closing paragraph of his introduction he suggests certain witnesses to this truth: first, John the Baptist, and then John the evangelist speaking in behalf of his fellow disciples and of all who have faith in Christ. (Vs. 15-16.)

Then, too, true to the supreme purpose of his Gospel, he shows how faith issues in life. Believers have all their spiritual needs supplied, and draw grace after grace from the inexhaustible "fulness" of Christ. This fullness is emphasized by contrast with the revelation granted through Moses, who gave a law but no power to obey, who set forth shadows the substance of which is found in Christ.

Thus the Prologue reaches its climax as for the first time it mentions the historic title "Jesus Christ," and again asserts his unique personality as "the only begotten from the Father," the final declaration, revelation, interpretation of the unseen God.

Such then is the introduction which John gives to his Gospel story. In these eighteen verses he presents the sum of his whole message. They compress into a single, brief paragraph the essential truths which the following chapters unfold. They declare that the eternal God was manifested among men; they show how some received while others rejected him; above all, they indicate the life of light and love and abiding blessedness which issues from faith in him whom John proves to be the divine Christ, the Son of God.

II
THE REVELATION TO THE WORLD, AND THE DEVELOPMENT OF FAITH AND UNBELIEF

Chs. 1:19 to 12:50

A. THE PREPARATION Chs. 1:19 to 2:11

1. The Witness of the Forerunner. Ch. 1:19-34
2. The Witness of the First Followers. Ch. 1:35-51
3. The Witness of the First Miracle. Ch. 2:1-11

1. THE WITNESS OF THE FORERUNNER Ch. 1:19-34

When John the Baptist steps upon the scene, the dramatic action of the Gospel begins; and yet his mission and the two events which follow are really preparatory to the public ministry of Christ. In each of the three, the great ideas of the Gospel emerge, yet, by each of the three, one of these ideas is emphasized. The ministry of John deals with testimony; the securing of the first disciples illustrates the development of faith; and the miracle at Cana affords a symbol of the life in which faith was to issue.

19 And this is the witness of John, when the Jews sent unto him from Jerusalem priests and Levites to ask him, Who art thou? 20 And he confessed, and denied not; and he confessed, I am not the Christ. 21 And they asked him, What then? Art thou Elijah? And he saith, I am not. Art thou the prophet? And he answered, No. 22 They said therefore unto him, Who art thou? that we may give

an answer to them that sent us. What sayest thou of thy-
self? 23 He said, I am the voice of one crying in the wil-
derness, Make straight the way of the Lord, as said Isaiah
the prophet. 24 And they had been sent from the Phari-
sees. 25 And they asked him, and said unto him, Why
then baptizest thou, if thou art not the Christ, neither Eli-
jah, neither the prophet? 26 John answered them, saying,
I baptize in water: in the midst of you standeth one whom
ye know not, 27 even he that cometh after me, the latchet
of whose shoe I am not worthy to unloose. 28 These
things were done in Bethany beyond the Jordan, where
John was baptizing.

Our Lord once declared: "Among them that are born
of women there hath not arisen a greater than John the
Baptist." He did not refer to the majesty of his character,
but to the dignity of his mission. John was the forerunner, the herald, of the Messiah. That such is the view-
point of this Gospel is intimated in the words by which
the ministry of the Baptist is introduced: "And this is the
witness of John." The writer is not concerned with the
dress, or personal habits, or eloquence, or moral grandeur,
of the great prophet but with his testimony to Christ. This
is given in two paragraphs.

In verses 19-28 is recorded the testimony that the
Messiah had come, unrecognized by his people; verses
29-34 give the witness to Jesus as being the Messiah.

The fame of John had filled the land; some persons
were even suggesting that the great preacher was the predicted Christ. The rulers could no longer disregard the
influence and power of the popular prophet. A deputa-
tion was sent to ask John who he claimed to be. He at
once declared that he was not the Christ; that he was not
Elijah who was expected to return to earth as the herald
of the Messiah; he was not "the prophet" of whom Moses
had spoken, and who was popularly related to the Messiah.

To this negative testimony about himself John now adds
the positive statement that he has come to prepare the

way for the Messiah by his call to repentance. This he expresses by a quotation from Isaiah: "The voice of one crying in the wilderness, Make straight the way of the Lord." John humbly calls himself a "voice," which is expressing a word, or is to testify to "the Word"; but he is claiming the dignity of fulfilling the prophecy of Isaiah, and authority as the appointed herald of the Messiah.

The delegation has another question to ask: If John is not the Christ, nor Elijah, nor "the prophet," why does he baptize? The reply is full of solemn significance: He is baptizing because the Christ is already standing in the midst of them. John is preparing men to receive him. He is himself unworthy to act as the humblest servant of this great Savior to whom he is bearing witness.

We can hardly resist drawing the parallel for today. Christ is still near, and unrecognized, and only his messengers and those who repent of sin will find him.

> *29 On the morrow he seeth Jesus coming unto him, and saith, Behold, the Lamb of God, that taketh away the sin of the world! 30 This is he of whom I said, After me cometh a man who is become before me: for he was before me. 31 And I knew him not; but that he should be made manifest to Israel, for this cause came I baptizing in water. 32 And John bare witness, saying, I have beheld the Spirit descending as a dove out of heaven; and it abode upon him. 33 And I knew him not: but he that sent me to baptize in water, he said unto me, Upon whomsoever thou shalt see the Spirit descending, and abiding upon him, the same is he that baptizeth in the Holy Spirit. 34 And I have seen, and have borne witness that this is the Son of God.*

The testimony so far recorded has been of significance because of its official character. It was given to a commission from the Jewish rulers; but, on the day following, public witness of a still more startling character is given by the Baptist. He points to Jesus and declares of him, "Behold, the Lamb of God, that taketh away the sin of the world!" It is totally inadequate to interpret the phrase "the Lamb of God" as denoting merely "the meekness and innocence of Christ." As the sin bearer, the Lamb must denote sacrifice, for there is no other way by which sin can be taken away. The verse brings us at once to the fifty-third chapter of Isaiah, where we see one suffering in the place of sinners; it transports us into the whole realm of Old Testament symbolism, and cannot be understood save in the light of offerings, and expiation, and atonement. It points us forward to the cross, and to the work of the Messiah who "bare our sins in his body upon the tree."

John further indicates the sign by which he is himself assured of the identity of the Messiah. It was he upon whom he had seen "the Spirit descending, and abiding upon him." John had previously known Jesus; but he had not known him as the Christ until this divinely promised sign had been fulfilled. In view of this spiritual anointing John gives his second great word of testimony: "This is the Son of God." By this phrase he indicated the unique, divine Personality of which mention had been made by the Evangelist in the Prologue. "He was before me," says John; yet John was born first. The Christ to whom he testifies had existed, therefore, before his birth; he had been "in the beginning . . . with God"; he "was God."

John further testifies that as "the Son of God," Jesus has power to baptize "in the Holy Spirit." Here John contrasts his own work with the work of Christ. John could baptize with water, he could perform a mere outward rite; but to true penitents, who trusted in him, Christ would give an inner, actual, supernatural, spiritual renewal. Water baptism by his herald was but a symbol of the purifying and transforming power of Christ.

Such was the witness of John the Baptist. When his ministry, as recorded here, is compared with the narrative of the other Gospels, it is noticeable how this writer is accomplishing his first specific aim, which is to prove "that Jesus is the Christ, the Son of God."

Is it not true that the very essence of the testimony which today should be borne to Christ concerns his divine Person and his saving work?

2. THE WITNESS OF THE FIRST FOLLOWERS
Ch. 1:35-51

35 Again on the morrow John was standing, and two of his disciples; 36 and he looked upon Jesus as he walked, and saith, Behold, the Lamb of God! 37 And the two disciples heard him speak, and they followed Jesus. 38 And Jesus turned, and beheld them following, and saith unto them, What seek ye? And they said unto him, Rabbi (which is to say, being interpreted, Teacher), where abidest thou? 39 He saith unto them, Come, and ye shall see. They came therefore and saw where he abode; and they abode with him that day: it was about the tenth hour. 40 One of the two that heard John speak, and followed him, was Andrew, Simon Peter's brother. 41 He findeth first his own brother Simon, and saith unto him, We have found the Messiah (which is, being interpreted, Christ). 42 He brought him unto Jesus. Jesus looked upon him, and said, Thou art Simon the son of John: thou shalt be called Cephas (which is by interpretation, Peter).

43 On the morrow he was minded to go forth into Galilee, and he findeth Philip: and Jesus saith unto him, Follow me. 44 Now Philip was from Bethsaida, of the city of Andrew and Peter. 45 Philip findeth Nathanael, and saith unto him, We have found him, of whom Moses in the law, and the prophets, wrote, Jesus of Nazareth, the son of Joseph. 46 And Nathanael said unto him, Can any good thing come out of Nazareth? Philip saith unto him, Come and see. 47 Jesus saw Nathanael coming to him, and saith of him, Behold, an Israelite indeed, in whom is no guile! 48 Nathanael saith unto him, Whence knowest thou me? Jesus answered and said unto him, Before Philip called thee, when thou wast under the fig tree, I saw thee. 49 Nathanael answered him, Rabbi, thou art the Son of

God; thou art King of Israel. *50 Jesus answered and said unto him, Because I said unto thee, I saw thee underneath the fig tree, believest thou? thou shalt see greater things than these.* *51 And he saith unto him, Verily, verily, I say unto you, Ye shall see the heaven opened, and the angels of God ascending and descending upon the Son of man.*

If the three great ideas of this Gospel are testimony, faith, and life, and if the first is introduced by the witness of John the Baptist, the second is surely emphasized in this narrative of the call of the first disciples. Here we see emerging the two other ideas also, but we are particularly concerned with the birth of faith. We find it to be in its essence the acceptance of testimony; and this paragraph is linked to the preceding by the fact that it was the testimony of John the Baptist which secured for Christ his first followers. Faith, however, becomes vital and active when it has brought one into personal contact with Christ; and this story shows how men who believe are ready to bear testimony, and how faith issues in life.

In the narrative of the witness of John, no specific mention was made of the result of his witness, yet we seemed instinctively to feel the sullen, silent unbelief of the Jewish rulers. That unbelief becomes a foil with which is contrasted the ready faith of honest, simple, inquiring souls.

Those who were the first to become disciples of Christ were Andrew and Peter, Philip and Nathanael, and probably James and the author of this Gospel, John.

Of the four distinctly named, it is interesting to note how in each case faith is awakened by testimony of a slightly different character. All were probably disciples of John the Baptist, and, as already indicated, the story of his witness is followed logically by this account of the first believers. Yet it is of Andrew that we read that he was one of the two disciples of John who heard him declare Jesus to be "the Lamb of God," and who consequently followed him. So, through the ages, the first form of testimony which has been securing followers for Christ is that of public speakers, in response to whose appeals faith has been awakened in the hearts of hearers. The prophetic office has never ceased. Today men like John the Baptist are needed, who with courage and consecration can stand before the multitudes and declare of Christ: "This is the Son of God. . . . Behold, the Lamb of God!"

In striking contrast, Peter became a disciple when testimony was brought to him by "his own brother." This personal witness to relatives and kindred is the most difficult form of all; it is also the most forcible and the most fruitful. There is a present and abiding need of more faithfulness as witnesses in the home circle and in the secrecy of private life.

Philip became a disciple in response to a direct call from Christ. In the narrative, this is the simplest and briefest statement of all; the parallel in modern life is more mysterious, but none the less real. There are countless Christians who have yielded themselves as followers of Christ because of an appeal which has been made by his Spirit directly to the heart. The mind of Philip had been prepared by the things he had already heard of Jesus. So these Christians have previously learned of the character and claims of Christ; but the final appeal and the act of decision have occurred at a time when they were alone with the Lord.

In the case of Nathanael, inquiry was first awakened by the word of a friend, who testified with deep conviction, and who turned Nathanael in the direction of faith by his memorable words, "Come and see." To turn resolutely toward Christ with open mind, to find out for ourselves what he is and claims to be, to enter the path of personal experience: this is for most men the avenue of faith.

Nathanael was a man of absolute sincerity, and when assured that Jesus of Nazareth was the Messiah, he voices an honest difficulty; he does not cast a slur upon the city where Jesus had been dwelling, as has commonly been supposed; but he knows that Nazareth was not the predicted birthplace of the Messiah, and he asks in surprise whether so great a thing can possibly come from Nazareth. His difficulty, however, does not cause inaction: he comes to Christ, to see for himself. The word of the Master at once shows Nathanael that a divine insight has read the very thoughts of his heart, and he cries out in adoration: "Rabbi, thou art the Son of God; thou art King of Israel."

Such are some of the various forms of testimony by which faith is awakened in the heart. It is for us to be fearless, honest, humble; to obey the call however it may be voiced, and to follow on to ever deeper conviction of the claims and powers of Christ.

It is equally interesting to note how these four men, so variously called, all became witnesses for Christ. John always brings actors upon the scene that they may bear testimony. The words of these first followers are arranged in a striking climax. First they call Christ "Rabbi," i.e., Master, or Teacher, suggesting, at least, that they are willing to be his disciples. Then they declare him to be "the Messiah," and, further, that he has been set forth both by the symbols of "the law" and the writings of "the prophets." Lastly, Nathanael declares him to be "the Son of God" as well as the Messiah, the "King of Israel."

The greatest of all the witnesses is Christ himself. The testimony reaches its climax when he calls himself "the Son of man." Too commonly it is regarded as a term contrasted with "the Son of God," and signifying the mere humanity of Christ. It does indeed signify the ideal, true man, but it is the title which is taken from Daniel, and indicates the Messiah who was one day to appear in divine glory, to whom was to be given a universal and eternal Kingdom.

The fact that those in whom faith is born themselves become witnesses to Christ suggests to us the third great truth of this Gospel which emerges in this narrative. Faith issues in life. This is what John always is showing. This is what he wishes to secure. He has written that we may believe, "that believing ye may have life." So as Simon comes to Christ, weak, impulsive, fickle, passionate, he is met with the promise: "Thou shalt be called Cephas," a stone. If one really believes in Christ, the result will be a complete transformation of character; instead of weakness there will be strength, courage, endurance, true manhood.

Nathanael confesses his faith and the response is given: "Ye shall see the heaven opened, and the angels of God ascending and descending upon the Son of man."

To the sincere seeker after truth there comes the promise of enlarged spiritual vision. To one who believes there comes the assurance that there will be found in Christ the union of man and God, and through him the restored communion between earth and heaven. Probably Nathanael had been thinking of Jacob's vision at Bethel, and wondering how and when he should catch the vision for which he longed, and by which his problems would be solved. There comes to him the promise that all he seeks can be had in Christ. It is the message echoed by Browning, "I say the acknowledgment of God in Christ, accepted by the reason, solves for thee all questions in the world and out of it."

3. THE WITNESS OF THE FIRST MIRACLE
Ch. 2:1-11

1 And the third day there was a marriage in Cana of Galilee; and the mother of Jesus was there: 2 and Jesus also was bidden, and his disciples, to the marriage. 3 And when the wine failed, the mother of Jesus saith unto him, They have no wine. 4 And Jesus saith unto her, Woman, what have I to do with thee? mine hour is not yet come. 5 His mother saith unto the servants, Whatsoever he saith unto you, do it. 6 Now there were six waterpots of stone set there after the Jews' manner of purifying, containing two or three firkins apiece. 7 Jesus saith unto them, Fill the waterpots with water. And they filled them up to the brim. 8 And he saith unto them, Draw out now, and bear unto the ruler of the feast. And they bare it. 9 And when the ruler of the feast tasted the water now become wine, and knew not whence it was (but the servants that had drawn the water knew), the ruler of the feast calleth the bridegroom, 10 and saith unto him, Every man setteth on first the good wine; and when men *have drunk freely,* then *that which is worse: thou hast kept the good wine until now. 11 This beginning of his signs did Jesus in Cana of Galilee, and manifested his glory; and his disciples believed on him.*

The ministry of John the Baptist, the call of the first disciples, and the miracle of Cana, which together form a section of the Gospel preparatory to the portrayal of the public ministry of our Lord, are narrated as occupying exactly a full week; what is more significant, they successively illustrate all the three dominant themes of the Gospel, namely, testimony to Christ, the development of faith, the transformation of life. The last is, of course, the supreme message of this charming story; yet the other thoughts emerge; and the account of this first miracle, or "sign," suggests how inseparable all these three truths are from each of the miracles of our Lord. Each testifies to his character, each awakes or confirms faith, each suggests the life which faith secures.

a. That this miracle was witness to the Person of Christ is stated in the eleventh verse: "This beginning of his signs did Jesus . . . , and manifested his glory." Each miracle related by John was intended to prove that Jesus was the Christ, the Son of God. Here, as our Lord turns water into wine, he shows himself "Ruler of all nature." It was an act of creation. It declared that in him God was present.

No miracle of Christ, however, was wrought simply as a prodigy, to appeal to the minds of spectators. There was always present the motive of love and sympathy.

Christ was here relieving embarrassment, he was giving joy, he was bestowing upon the bridegroom a gift of no inconsiderable value. He was suggesting that his nature was loving, sympathetic, divine; "his glory" was the glory of the God who is love. He was the Son of God.

Even in the dialogue with his mother, which we find difficult to explain fully, there is further testimony to his Person. As he calls her "woman," there is indicated no lack of respect or even of affection; the title was often used in addressing persons of rank. Nor was there anything of harshness in the words that follow: "What have I to do with thee? mine hour is not yet come"; yet there is here the definite intimation that he was the Christ.

What Mary seemed to desire was that her Son should take this occasion to manifest himself openly as the Messiah, and she mentions the need of wine as her reason for suggesting such a Messianic manifestation. He knows that this is not the time or the place; it must be at the Passover and in Jerusalem. His "hour" had "not yet come." He fulfills the need of the guests, he grants the request of his mother, while denying, and mildly, lovingly rebuking the deeper, larger desire of her heart. Yet in his denial he is admitting the truth that he is the Messiah, and that, as such, he will soon appear.

May we not add that the very symbolism of the marriage feast, and the joy which Jesus brought to the wedding hour, suggested the Messianic symbolism of the Old Testament, and the presence among men of him whom John the Baptist called the Bridegroom. Thus in this "beginning of . . . signs" the Evangelist is producing testimony to prove that Jesus is both "the Christ" and "the Son of God."

b. This testimony is further related, as are all the subsequent "signs," to belief. We read that, as a result of the miracle, "his disciples believed on him." They had believed on him before; at least they had believed him. By this miracle their faith was strengthened and confirmed.

They now trusted in him, their doubts were removed, they committed themselves to him without question or reserve.

This result should be noted in the case of all the recorded miracles. They were not intended, and surely did not result, in merely arousing interest or faith in the minds of the indifferent or the skeptical; they likewise made their appeal to disciples, and developed and established their belief.

The experience of those first believers is ours. First there is an incipient faith based upon the testimony of others; then there is the larger confidence due to personal contact with Christ; and then there comes the more perfect faith resulting from personal experience and observation of the power and works of our Lord.

c. The deepest meaning of the miracle relates, however, to the life of believers. All the "signs" wrought by our Lord were symbolic of the experiences which would result from faith in him; it is most significant, therefore, that his first miracle, which was an index to his whole ministry, was so related to the joy of a wedding feast. It rebukes the foolish fear that religion robs life of its happiness, or that loyalty to Christ is inconsistent with exuberant spirits and innocent pleasure. It corrects the false impression that sourness is a sign of sainthood, or that gloom is a condition of godliness. It indicates the transforming, ennobling, transfiguring power of Christ, and shows how he came that we "may have life, and may have it abundantly."

It may be true, as certain ancient writers suggest, that the miracle pictured the changing of Jewish forms and ceremonies into the substance and realities of Christian truth; but it is certain that, by his presence at the wedding and his part in the feast, our Lord showed his approval of joy and gladness; he sanctified marriage and all our social relationships; and above all, he indicated how human lives would be glorified by him, and the characters and capacities of his followers be brought to their highest

development and their fullest possibilities.   It is for us to
show the obedience of true faith; his work may be done
in divine silence; we are to heed the word spoken by Mary
to the servants: "Whatsoever he saith unto you, do it."

B. THE PUBLIC MINISTRY Chs. 2:12 to 12:50

1. THE OPENING OF THE MINISTRY
Chs. 2:12 to 4:54

a. The Witness in Jerusalem.   Chs. 2:12 to 3:21
b. The Witness in Judea.   Ch. 3:22-36
c. The Witness in Samaria.   Ch. 4:1-42
d. The Witness in Galilee.   Ch. 4:43-54

a. The Witness in Jerusalem   Chs. 2:12 to 3:21

(1) The Witness in the Temple   Ch. 2:12-22

*12 After this he went down to Capernaum, he, and his
mother, and his brethren, and his disciples; and there they
abode not many days.*

*13 And the passover of the Jews was at hand, and Jesus
went up to Jerusalem.   14 And he found in the temple
those that sold oxen and sheep and doves, and the changers
of money sitting: 15 and he made a scourge of cords, and
cast all out of the temple, both the sheep and the oxen;
and he poured out the changers' money, and overthrew
their tables; 16 and to them that sold the doves he said,
Take these things hence; make not my Father's house a
house of merchandise.   17 His disciples remembered that
it was written, Zeal for thy house shall eat me up.   18 The
Jews therefore answered and said unto him, What sign
showest thou unto us, seeing that thou doest these things?
19 Jesus answered and said unto them, Destroy this temple, and in three days I will raise it up.   20 The Jews
therefore said, Forty and six years was this temple in build-
ing, and wilt thou raise it up in three days?   21 But he
spake of the temple of his body.   22 When therefore he
was raised from the dead, his disciples remembered that he*

spake this; and they believed the scripture, and the word which Jesus had said.

There was but one place and time for our Lord to inaugurate fittingly his public ministry; it must be at the capital city, and in the Temple, the very center of life and worship; it must be at the Passover feast, the most solemn period of the year, and the season when the city would be thronged with pilgrims from every quarter of the globe. There and then he could offer himself to the people as their Messiah, in whom were to be realized all the types and hopes suggested by the great national festival.

The story is prefaced by a brief statement which is not wanting in significance: "After this he went down to Capernaum, he, and his mother, and his brethren, and his disciples; and there they abode not many days." (V. 12.) Jesus was waiting for the Passover; he knew always when his "hour" was come; he was also selecting a more convenient center than Nazareth for his public ministry. This verse marks the transition from his private to his public career.

On the eve of the Passover, Jesus appears in Jerusalem and presents himself as the Messiah by an act of deep symbolic import. He drives from the Temple the traders by whom the place of divine worship has been defiled. He comes as the Son of God, filled with zeal for his Father's house. He comes as the Messiah of Israel, offering to secure national purification which will preface the Messianic Kingdom and blessedness.

The abuse which our Lord was rebuking had arisen from what was at first a mere matter of convenience for worshipers. The sale of sacrifices in a place adjacent to the Temple, and the exchange of foreign money for the sacred coins with which the Temple tax could be paid, was all innocent enough; but little by little the traffic had crowded into the very court of the Temple; it was accompanied by disorder, greed, dishonesty, and extortion, until the place of worship had become, as Christ declared, "a house of merchandise."

Our Lord takes a scourge of cords, not as an instrument of offense but as a badge of authority, and expels the traders, declaring that the Temple is his Father's house. In no other more definite or picturesque way could he have asserted his claim to be the Christ, the Son of God.

The significance of the act is at once appreciated by the disciples who, at least, see in this incident the fulfillment of a Messianic prophecy: "Zeal for thy house shall eat me up."

On the other hand the rulers regard the action with sullen unbelief or with a sense of offended dignity; they demand of Christ a "sign" in justification of what he has done and as a proof of the divine authority he is claiming to possess. Their demand was a stupid impertinence. It was like asking for proof of a proof. His act was itself a sign which they should have interpreted.

Jesus does promise, however, a sign so significant that in its light no man would henceforth have any excuse for doubting that he was "the Christ, the Son of God." He declares that his death and resurrection are to be the unanswerable arguments as to his divine Person and mission.

He phrases his reply, however, in such language that, for the time, not even his disciples are able to comprehend his meaning: "Destroy this temple, and in three days I will raise it up." "He spake of the temple of his body," the writer explains. The Jews thought he referred to the literal Temple, and received his words with contemptuous incredulity. After his resurrection "his disciples remembered that he spake this; and they believed the scripture, and the word which Jesus had said." It is in the light of the resurrection that we can understand the Bible, and can interpret and believe the words and claims of Christ.

It is noticeable that Jesus began his ministry with an act of holiness rather than of power. He wished to teach the nation that the supreme need was their spiritual cleansing, their purification as worshipers, their moral elevation as the people of God; and he wished to suggest that he could bring such blessings if they would accept and follow him.

It is further noticeable that Jesus saw, in the unbelief manifested in the first hour of his ministry, the certainty of his final rejection and the clear vision of the cross. They who would not receive him would indeed destroy the "temple of his body." He saw, however, his resurrection, and all that it would imply and secure. It would forever be the supreme justification of his claims; but, further, as his death involved the destruction of the literal Temple and its worship, so his resurrection would secure the erection of a truer spiritual temple, even the church of Christ; and in place of a ritual of forms and shadows and types, there would rise a religion of truer worship and of more real fellowship with God.

We see then in this narrative the familiar ideas of this Gospel, testimony to the truth that Jesus is the Christ, the Son of God, the response of unbelief and of faith, and the issue of faith in life, here pictured as the enjoyment of all those realities which the ancient Temple symbolized and foreshadowed.

(2) The Witness of Miracles   Ch. 2:23-25

23 Now when he was in Jerusalem at the passover, during the feast, many believed on his name, beholding his signs which he did. 24 But Jesus did not trust himself unto them, for that he knew all men, 25 and because he needed not that any one should bear witness concerning man; for he himself knew what was in man.

During the seven days' celebration of the feast, Jesus remains in Jerusalem, and arouses curiosity, wonder, and even incipient faith, by performing certain miracles. "Many believed on his name"; they were willing to accept him as a Worker of miracles, "beholding his signs which he did," but they did not really trust him or commit themselves to him as Master and Lord; they did not believe in him as "the Christ, the Son of God." Then we read, "Jesus did not trust himself unto them, for that he knew all men." He who could read the heart was not deceived by any mere external appearances, or outward professions. He could distinguish between partial and real faith; and to those who are not willing to commit themselves to him and to trust him wholly he never reveals himself in all his fullness.

Even this minute paragraph is molded by the dominant ideas of the Gospel. Testimony is borne by "signs," faith is awakened, and it is suggested that where it is sincere, and develops into trust, there will issue the life which results in an ever-deepening knowledge of Christ.

Thus, too, these verses form the link between the preceding and the following striking narratives. The former shows the absolute unbelief of the rulers, and the true faith of the disciples; the latter pictures a ruler whose faith is only the incipient, imperfect belief of those who accept Christ as a Worker of miracles; but as he is sincere his faith deepens, Christ does reveal himself to him, and the ruler becomes also the disciple.

(3) The Witness to Nicodemus   Ch. 3:1-21

1 Now there was a man of the Pharisees, named Nicodemus, a ruler of the Jews: 2 the same came unto him by night, and said to him, Rabbi, we know that thou art a teacher come from God; for no one can do these signs that thou doest, except God be with him. 3 Jesus answered and said unto him, Verily, verily, I say unto thee, Except one be born anew, he cannot see the kingdom of God. 4 Nicodemus saith unto him, How can a man be born when he is old? can he enter a second time into his mother's womb, and be born? 5 Jesus answered, Verily, verily, I say unto thee, Except one be born of water and the Spirit, he cannot enter into the kingdom of God. 6 That which is born of the flesh is flesh; and that which is born of the Spirit is spirit.   7 Marvel not that I said unto thee, Ye must be born anew.   8 The wind bloweth where it will, and thou hearest the voice thereof, but knowest not whence it cometh, and whither it goeth: so is every one that is born of the Spirit.   9 Nicodemus answered and said unto him, How can these things be?   10 Jesus answered and said unto him, Art thou the teacher of Israel, and understandest not these things?   11 Verily, verily, I say unto thee, We speak that which we know, and bear witness of that which we have seen; and ye receive not our witness.   12 If I told you earthly things and ye believe not, how shall ye believe if I tell you heavenly things?   13 And no one hath ascended into heaven, but he that descended out of heaven, even the Son of man, who is in heaven.   14 And as Moses lifted up the serpent in the wilderness, even so must the Son of man be lifted up; 15 that whosoever believeth may in him have eternal life.

16 For God so loved the world, that he gave his only begotten Son, that whosoever believeth on him should not perish, but have eternal life.   17 For God sent not the Son into the world to judge the world; but that the world should be saved through him.   18 He that believeth on him is not judged: he that believeth not hath been judged already, because he hath not believed on the name of the only begotten Son of God.   19 And this is the judgment, that the light is come into the world, and men loved the darkness rather than the light; for their works were evil.   20 For every one that doeth evil hateth the light, and cometh not to the light, lest his works should be reproved.   21 But he that doeth the truth cometh to the light, that his works may be made manifest, that they have been wrought in God.

There is an unfailing charm in the story of Nicodemus but also a deep undertone of pathos and sadness. His character is sketched in three scenes: in the first he appears as a cautious inquirer, in the second, as a timid defender, in the third, as a secret disciple of Christ. He was a Pharisee, but not therefore a hypocrite. The Pharisees, in spite of their formalism, composed the most popular and most patriotic party in Jerusalem, and among them were men of earnestness and piety. He was "a ruler," i.e., a member of the Sanhedrin, a man of high reputation, of learning, of influence, of power; and the story suggests to us the great service he might have rendered to the Master had he not been so evidently lacking in moral courage.

He came to Jesus "by night"; nevertheless he came: that is the important point. The time may indicate timidity, but the fact, and the sequel, reveal sincerity. The great "teacher of Israel" came to the despised Prophet from Galilee, seeking for light; and because of his sincerity Jesus revealed to him the marvelous truths concerning his Person and his saving work.

There may have been something of presumption, of self-sufficiency, of pedantry, about the words with which he opens the interview: "Rabbi, we know that thou art a teacher come from God; for no one can do these signs that thou doest, except God be with him"; but there was something more serious still, which needed correction, in the mind and heart of the inquirer, as was shown by the startling reply of our Lord: "Verily, verily, I say unto thee, Except one be born anew, he cannot see the kingdom of God."

Nicodemus sincerely longed for the coming of that Kingdom, but he expected it to be established by a political revolution, and by acts of power, which the miracles of Christ seemed to prophesy; and he believed that every Jew, by right of birth, would have a place in that Kingdom.

It was surprising to be told that even he must experience a new birth, in order to enter and enjoy the blessings of the Kingdom, and his reply expresses his astonishment: "How can a man be born when he is old?" Probably he was interpreting the words with stupid literalism, as referring to a physical birth; but possibly he understands the reference of our Lord to a moral renewal, and borrows his figure to express the objection so familiar in these modern days: "Character is the product of countless past impressions and experiences; it cannot begin anew." Whatever the false impression of Nicodemus may have been, his ideas were moving wholly in the sphere of the material or the natural, and Christ proceeds, therefore, to emphasize the truth of the spiritual and the divine, as he explains to him fully what he means by the new birth. How difficult it is for men to take a spiritual view of life, and to understand that "the kingdom of God" can never be brought in by political expedients and social reforms and natural processes; but that the first great need is a renewal of the heart and a divine transformation of each individual man. "Jesus answered Verily, verily, I say unto thee, Except one be born of water and the Spirit, he cannot enter into the kingdom of God."

By "water" Jesus referred to the baptism of John and to similar rites with which Nicodemus was familiar. There must be repentance, confession, pardon, purification from sin, before one could be prepared to enter the Kingdom; but there must be something more. There must be the renewing and transforming power of the Spirit of God. Mere human nature, however beautiful, or cultured, or sincere, can never rise above itself, or produce anything better than itself. It possesses, however, capacities for a higher life, which can be awakened, and called into operation only by the Spirit of God: "That which is born of the flesh is flesh; and that which is born of the Spirit is spirit." The truth is so obvious that it should occasion us no surprise: "Marvel not that I said unto thee, Ye must be born anew."

There is, however, a mystery about the new birth, as about every act of God. One who is born of the Spirit is like the wind. We cannot tell its direction or source, yet we can see its effects. It is the manifestation of an unseen power. So the life of the regenerate soul will always be a puzzle and an enigma to men of the world; yet even they must be able to test its genuineness by its acts of humility, of purity, of love.

As Nicodemus expresses his surprise or bewilderment, our Lord states that these are truths which he should have already known; they are merely "earthly things," which the Old Testament taught, and John had recently proclaimed; but there are "heavenly things" concerning Jesus' own Person and work which he alone can reveal. These "heavenly things" do not concern the need and nature of the new birth, which Nicodemus should already have known, but they declare its condition, its method, even faith in a divine, crucified Savior; they answer the eager question of Nicodemus: "How can these things be?" These last words must express more than blind incredulity or astonishment. Nicodemus must have been willing to believe; for Christ now proceeds to reveal to him in startling fullness the divine plan of salvation. He assures Nicodemus that he is worthy of trust as he brings the revelation, for he is not only a human messenger "sent from God" but a divine Being, one with God, who came down from heaven, and, even as man, is in the most full and free and perfect fellowship with God.

The substance of the revelation is this: "As Moses lifted up the serpent in the wilderness, even so must the Son of man be lifted up; that whosoever believeth may in him have eternal life."

What a striking use Christ here makes of a story from Old Testament history; and with what divine prevision does he foresee his own death upon the cross! The figure is not to be pressed in all of its possible details; yet we should here note the suggestions: (1) Men are, like the Israelites of old, serpent-bitten; but the deadly poison is the sting of sin. (2) God has provided a remedy in the Person of his Son; in his crucifixion we see sin vanquished, as the uplifted serpent pictured the death of the destroyer; yet, as the uplifted serpent was not real, but one of brass, so Christ was not really a partaker of sin but only made "in the likeness of sinful flesh." (3) As it was necessary for the dying Israelite to accept God's provision, and, with submission and faith, to look upon the brazen serpent, so it is necessary for us to look, in repentance and faith, to the crucified Savior, and to commit ourselves to God as he is graciously revealed in Jesus Christ. If we refuse to accept Christ we "perish," but faith results in "eternal life." (4) This provision is made by the love of God, and is freely offered to everyone who will believe: "For God so loved the world, that he gave his only begotten Son, that whosoever believeth on him should not perish, but have eternal life."

The question is often raised as to whether verses 16-21 are the words of Jesus, or of John. It is not a problem of supreme consequence, for whether uttered by our Lord in the presence of Nicodemus or embodying truth taught to John on other occasions, they form a fitting conclusion to this fascinating narrative. The preceding verses have recorded the testimony to the Person of Christ, as "a teacher come from God," as "the Son of man" who descended out of heaven, who hath ascended into heaven, who is the Savior of all who believe in him; they have further shown that faith results in life, in being "born anew"; in salvation, in having "eternal life." This closing paragraph contains, in verse sixteen, a summary of the Gospel, further testifying to the Person of Christ as the "only begotten Son" of God, but, in this verse and in the verses following, it deals particularly with the third great theme of the Evangelist, namely, faith. Here stress is laid upon the moral element in belief or unbelief. It is declared that the great purpose of God in sending Christ into the world is to save men; but that those who reject him place themselves under condemnation. As he is holy and pure and divine, those who turn from him must do so because they love sin. They are not willing to live in the presence of him who is "the true light" and who, as such, would rebuke the works of darkness. Christ is still the touchstone of character.

On the other hand, there are always those who are sincere and true, who desire to come to the light. For them there is divine approval; to them comes more light. That Nicodemus was of the latter class his subsequent history shows. This first interview with the Master may well have closed with some such word of approval and encourage-ment and hope.

b. The Witness in Judea   Ch. 3:22-36

22 After these things came Jesus and his disciples into the land of Judæa; and there he tarried with them, and baptized. 23 And John also was baptizing in Ænon near to Salim, because there was much water there: and they came, and were baptized. 24 For John was not yet cast into prison. 25 There arose therefore a questioning on the part of John's disciples with a Jew about purifying. 26 And they came unto John, and said to him, Rabbi, he that was with thee beyond the Jordan, to whom thou hast borne wit-ness, behold, the same baptizeth, and all men come to him. 27 John answered and said, A man can receive nothing, except it have been given him from heaven. 28 Ye your-selves bear me witness, that I said, I am not the Christ, but, that I am sent before him. 29 He that hath the bride is the bridegroom: but the friend of the bridegroom, that stand-eth and heareth him, rejoiceth greatly because of the bride-groom's voice: this my joy therefore is made full. 30 He must increase, but I must decrease.

31 He that cometh from above is above all: he that is of the earth is of the earth, and of the earth he speaketh: he that cometh from heaven is above all. 32 What he hath seen and heard, of that he beareth witness; and no man receiveth his witness. 33 He that hath received his witness hath set his seal to this, that God is true. 34 For he whom God hath sent speaketh the words of God: for he giveth not the Spirit by measure. 35 The Father loveth the Son, and hath given all things into his hand. 36 He that believeth on the Son hath eternal life; but he that obeyeth not the Son shall not see life, but the wrath of God abideth on him.

Jesus now withdraws from Jerusalem. He has been re-ceived with coldness and unbelief. He continues his ministry in Judea, but outside the capital city. His work for the present is that of teaching his disciples, and, by their hands, administering baptism to new followers. John the Baptist is laboring in the same vicinity, and not unnaturally the question is raised as to the relation between the work of Jesus and of John. An opportunity is thus afforded to John of delivering his final and supreme witness to Christ. Some suppose that the words of John end with the thirtieth verse, and others that they continue to the end of the chapter; but whether spoken by the Baptist or by the Evangelist the whole section embodies a striking testimony to the Person and work of our Lord, and a solemn warning as to the issues of faith and unbelief.

The immediate occasion of the witness of the Baptist was a remark of his disciples which evidenced something of jealousy: "Rabbi, he that was with thee beyond the Jordan, to whom thou hast borne witness, behold, the same baptizeth, and all men come to him." In noble contrast, John replies with deep and characteristic humility that the different tasks in life, and all apparent degrees of greatness, must be explained as the expression of the will of God, and that he is perfectly satisfied, nay, that he rejoices in the part assigned to him in relation to the work and ministry of Christ. John calls himself "the friend of the bridegroom," i.e., one who arranged the wedding contract and presided at the wedding feast and was glad as he heard the voice of the bridegroom's greeting. He declares his great joy at being privileged, as the actual forerunner of Christ, to prepare a people for the heavenly Bridegroom. Last of all he speaks that word which should be a motto for everyone in relation to the Master: "He must increase, but I must decrease."

So far the witness of the paragraph has been rather negative. It has shown the inferiority of John to Jesus, and the relation of their respective ministries. The closing words show the infinite superiority of Jesus to all men, and his unique relation to God.

Witness is borne (1) to the divine origin of Jesus: "He

that cometh from above is above all," which is a reference, not to the source of his mission, but to his Being. In virtue of such an origin, and in contrast with men, who are limited by the experiences of earth, his (2) teaching is absolutely authoritative, for he has been a witness of the heavenly truths he proclaims; and yet men are unwilling to receive his testimony. There are exceptions, however, and each believer has the dignity of being one who sets his seal to the veracity of God. To believe Christ is to believe God; for Christ speaks the very words of God; to him the Father has given his Spirit in all fullness, and not in limited measure as to human teachers. Nor is Christ merely a teacher; in virtue of his love, the Father has bestowed upon him, as his Son, (3) universal authority. He has "all authority . . . in heaven and on earth."

In view of such teaching and authority, the paragraph may well close with the solemn warning as to the eternal issues of faith and unbelief, which declares that belief on the Son of God assures the present and continued enjoyment of "eternal life," but that the rejection of the Son involves the experiencing of "the wrath of God."

c. The Witness in Samaria   Ch. 4:1-42

1 When therefore the Lord knew that the Pharisees had heard that Jesus was making and baptizing more disciples than John 2 (although Jesus himself baptized not, but his disciples), 3 he left Judæa, and departed again into Galilee. 4 And he must needs pass through Samaria. 5 So he cometh to a city of Samaria, called Sychar, near to the parcel of ground that Jacob gave to his son Joseph: 6 and Jacob's well was there. Jesus therefore, being wearied with his journey, sat thus by the well. It was about the sixth hour. 7 There cometh a woman of Samaria to draw water: Jesus saith unto her, Give me to drink. 8 For his disciples were gone away into the city to buy food. 9 The Samaritan woman therefore saith unto him, How is it that thou, being a Jew, askest drink of me, who am a Samaritan woman? (For Jews have no dealing with Samaritans.)   10 Jesus answered and said unto her, If thou knewest the gift of God, and who it is that saith to thee, Give me to drink; thou wouldest have asked of him, and he would have given thee living water. 11 The woman saith unto him, Sir, thou hast nothing to draw with, and the well is deep: whence then hast thou that living water? 12 Art thou greater than our father Jacob, who gave us the well, and drank thereof himself, and his sons, and his cattle? 13 Jesus answered and said unto her, Every one that drinketh of this water shall thirst again: 14 but whosoever drinketh of the water that I shall give him shall never thirst; but the water that I shall give him shall become in him a well of water springing up unto eternal life. 15 The woman saith unto him, Sir, give me this water, that I thirst not, neither come all the way hither to draw. 16 Jesus saith unto her, Go, call thy husband, and come hither. 17 The woman answered and said unto him, I have no husband. Jesus saith unto her, Thou saidst well, I have no husband: 18 for thou hast had five husbands; and he whom thou now hast is not thy husband: this hast thou said truly. 19 The woman saith unto him, Sir, I perceive that thou art a prophet. 20 Our fathers worshipped in this mountain; and ye say, that in Jerusalem is the place where men ought to worship. 21 Jesus saith unto her, Woman, believe me, the hour cometh, when neither in this mountain, nor in Jerusalem, shall ye worship the Father. 22 Ye worship that which ye know not: we worship that which we know; for salvation is from the Jews. 23 But the hour cometh, and now is, when the true worshippers shall worship the Father in spirit and truth: for such doth the Father seek to be his worshippers. 24 God is a Spirit: and they that worship him must worship in spirit and truth. 25 The woman saith unto him, I know that Messiah cometh (he that is called Christ): when he is come, he will declare unto us all things. 26 Jesus saith unto her, I that speak unto thee am he.

27 And upon this came his disciples; and they marvelled that he was speaking with a woman; yet no man said, What seekest thou? or, Why speakest thou with her? 28 So the woman left her waterpot, and went away into the city, and saith to the people, 29 Come, see a man, who told me all things that ever I did: can this be the Christ? 30 They

went out of the city, and were coming to him. 31 In the mean while the disciples prayed him, saying, Rabbi, eat. 32 But he said unto them, I have meat to eat that ye know not. 33 The disciples therefore said one to another, Hath any man brought him aught to eat? 34 Jesus saith unto them, My meat is to do the will of him that sent me, and to accomplish his work. 35 Say not ye, There are yet four months, and then cometh the harvest? behold, I say unto you, Lift up your eyes, and look on the fields, that they are white already unto harvest. 36 He that reapeth receiveth wages, and gathereth fruit unto life eternal; that he that soweth and he that reapeth may rejoice together. 37 For herein is the saying true, One soweth, and another reapeth. 38 I sent you to reap that whereon ye have not labored: others have labored, and ye are entered into their labor.

39 And from that city many of the Samaritans believed on him because of the word of the woman, who testified, He told me all things that ever I did. 40 So when the Samaritans came unto him, they besought him to abide with them: and he abode there two days. 41 And many more believed because of his word; 42 and they said to the woman, Now we believe, not because of thy speaking: for we have heard for ourselves, and know that this is indeed the Saviour of the world.

In striking contrast to the cold unbelief with which our Lord was received in Jerusalem and in Judea, was his experience in Samaria, where a whole city accepted him as the promised Messiah.

It was the more striking because he remained there only two days, while on his journey from Judea to Galilee, he performed there no miracles, and those who so readily received him regarded all of his race as their natural enemies.

It would be difficult to find a finer piece of dramatic writing than is contained in the dialogue between Jesus and the woman at Jacob's well, and in the subsequent narrative of her testimony to her fellow townsmen. To regard it as fiction is to credit John with miraculous literary skill. He must have seen and heard what is here recorded. Therefore, as a narrative of fact, it challenges our attention to notice what Christ claimed for himself, how he developed faith in those who were willing to receive his word, and what he promised to those who put their trust in him.

The narrative is full of encouragement for all who are sincerely seeking for light on religious problems; for it shows how faith may be gradually enlarged and strengthened. This woman looked upon Jesus, at first, as being merely a weary traveler, a Jew, then as "a prophet," and finally as the "Messiah" whom her townsmen call "the Saviour of the world."

Here, too, is great encouragement for all who are laboring as witnesses for Christ. They are assured of "fields, . . . white already unto harvest" if they are only ready to lift up their eyes, to speak to passing strangers, to testify where opportunities are offered.

Most of all is the story instructive to those who wish to learn the method of approach to the souls who are in need of Christ. We cannot, of course, follow the example of Christ exactly, in every case, appealing to just so many motives in his precise order; but we can find here illustrations of those attitudes of heart and mind to which we must appeal, if we are to bring men and women into vital fellowship with Christ, and into the enjoyment of that life which is promised to those who believe in him.

(1) We notice first of all that Christ makes a request appealing to sympathy. (Vs. 7-9.) "Give me to drink." Not only would the mention of his pitiful thirst touch the heart of a woman, but the fact that a Jew would ask drink of a Samaritan would indicate that he felt sympathy for her. In asking a favor, the petitioner, for the time, places himself upon a level with the person he addresses. He was a rabbi, but he was willing to speak to a woman, a poor woman who was performing the act of a servant, a woman who was a social outcast, a woman who belonged to a de-

spised race. The very fact that he should make a request of her made her willing to listen further to what he had to say. He won his way into her heart by his first word. He made her believe that something beside his thirst led him to address her. There are those who regard the woman as cynical, insulting, flippant. She is, rather, an example of the openhearted sincerity which is necessary in case we are to learn more from Christ. Only when we believe that he desires to help us, only when we feel something of sympathy for him, can he reveal himself to us. So, too, in approaching a needy soul with Christian testimony, we must be careful "to win at the start," to establish some common ground, to make it evident that we really desire to confer a benefit, that we feel true, unselfish interest.

(2) Christ also makes a claim appealing to curiosity. (Vs. 10-12.) If curiosity had been aroused already by his request, it is now fanned into a flame by the statement which falls from his lips: "If thou knewest the gift of God, and who it is that saith to thee, Give me to drink; thou wouldest have asked of him, and he would have given thee living water." That is the way to arouse curiosity: "If you knew; but of course you do not!" The woman at once is asking herself who he can be. Does he claim to be greater than Jacob who gave the well? What are the claims of Christ? What does he say of himself? Does he declare that he is more than man, even the divine Son of God? If men are to be saved, they must be brought seriously to consider exactly these questions. It is indifference which is so perilous. When a man is aroused to consider the words and the claims of Christ recorded in this Gospel, he is certain to find more light.

(3) Christ next makes a promise appealing to conscious need: "Whosoever drinketh of the water that I shall give him shall never thirst." (Vs. 13-15.) Satisfaction was exactly that for which this poor woman was longing. She had sought for it all her life, and in her search she had

been restrained by no laws of God or of man; but she was thirsting still, and the thirst would never be satisfied till she found in Christ a personal Lord and Savior.

Men need to know the claims of Christ; but they should hear his promise as well. There is in every heart a thirst, a sense of lack, which our Lord promises to satisfy. Really to know him and to trust him is to have within the heart "a well of water springing up unto eternal life."

All that Jesus meant and promised, the woman could not have understood; but in her eager reply we hear voiced the inarticulate cry of every human heart: "Sir, give me this water, that I thirst not, neither come all the way hither to draw."

(4) Jesus now gives a command appealing to the conscience: "Go, call thy husband, and come hither." Why this command? Because no matter how fully we may admit the claims of Christ, or how truly we may understand his promises, we can never find satisfaction and peace till we make right the thing in the life that is wrong. Jesus has put his finger on the sore spot in this life. She at once shrinks. Her answer is half true; it is made meditatively rather than in anger; the stranger has given a command which touches the dark secret of her soul. Not unnaturally she is heard to reply, "I have no husband."

(5) Jesus at once makes a disclosure appealing to the religious instinct. (Vs. 17-20.) He lays bare the whole story of her life, and in so doing reveals such divine insight that she at once calls him "a prophet," and asks him a question relative to the true place of worship. There are those who feel that she is shrewdly attempting to change the conversation which has become uncomfortably personal. But the connection of thought is evidently deeper. The revelation of her hidden life, and presence of a divine messenger, appeal to a religious instinct which however dormant is never dead. The woman thinks of religion, however, as a matter of form and ceremony. She has never found any satisfaction in its observances. So, with

some sincerity, she is asking the opinion of the prophet as to the proper place for religious rites.   Possibly, she thinks, the mistake has been here; should one worship at Mount Gerizim, as the Samaritans believed, or at Jerusalem, as the Jews taught?

(6) Our Lord now makes a revelation appealing to hope.   (Vs. 21-25.)   He tells the woman that her trouble has not been as to the place of worship, but as to the fact; she has never worshiped at all.   "God is a Spirit" and true worship is therefore not a question of place but of faith and love, not a matter of form and ceremony, but of spiritual reality; its essence is found in a true knowledge of God and in fellowship with him as a loving Father.   Jerusalem has indeed been the divinely appointed place of worship, related to the revelation of salvation made through the Jews, but the time has come when there are to be no local restrictions to worship.   True worshipers will not be concerned with place and symbol, but will worship "in spirit and truth."   That there is need of some Mediator to give this fuller knowledge of God, and to bring guilty souls into fellowship with him, is suggested by the immediate reply of the woman: "I know that Messiah cometh: . . . he will declare unto us all things."   Some hope of such a Savior had been kept alive in her heart, in spite of all her ignorance and sin.

(7) The woman is now ready for the supreme word. This was a declaration appealing to faith: "I that speak unto thee am he."   Does the woman believe?   Her action is more eloquent than speech.   Six times Jesus has addressed her and each time she has made a reply.   His seventh word declares him to be the Messiah; she makes no verbal answer, but we read that she "left her waterpot, and went away into the city, and saith to the people, Come, see a man, who told me all things that ever I did: can this be the Christ?"   We do not know just how perfect her faith may have been; but, today, when a man or woman is found so interested in Christ that the daily task is for a

time forgotten, and the one desire is to tell others about
Christ, we are safe to conclude that faith is real and vital.
As we read how this new disciple goes on her surprising
and successful mission, as we see the Samaritans coming
forth to welcome the Messiah, the narrative reaches its
climax of interest and inspiration.

In reply to the disciples who offered him food to eat,
Jesus declares that his deeper satisfaction lies in revealing
himself to fainting souls, as he has just done to the woman
at the well. Those who seek him are sure to be surprised
by the clear revelation of himself he delights to give.
(Vs. 31-34.)

As Jesus sees the Samaritans streaming forth to meet
him, because of the witness they have heard, Jesus intimates that opportunities for fruitful testimony are always
at hand for his followers. There is never reason for delay. The fields "are white already." It is as though
others had sown the seed of the harvests we may reap,
and our reward consists in the salvation of immortal souls.
(Vs. 35-38.)

As the Samaritans receive him gladly into their city and
their hearts, demanding no miracle, and trusting him simply because of his word, we catch a prophetic vision of
the multitudes from all nations who will be glad to welcome the Messiah whom the Jews are rejecting and to find
life in him whom they declare to be "the Saviour of the
world."   (Vs. 38-42.)

d. The Witness in Galilee   Ch. 4:43-54

*43 And after the two days he went forth from thence
into Galilee. 44 For Jesus himself testified, that a prophet
hath no honor in his own country. 45 So when he came
into Galilee, the Galilæans received him, having seen all
the things that he did in Jerusalem at the feast: for they also
went unto the feast.*

*46 He came therefore again unto Cana of Galilee, where
he made the water wine. And there was a certain noble-*

> *man, whose son was sick at Capernaum.   47 When he*
> *heard that Jesus was come out of Judæa into Galilee, he*
> *went unto him, and besought him that he would come*
> *down, and heal his son; for he was at the point of death.*
> *48 Jesus therefore said unto him, Except ye see signs and*
> *wonders, ye will in no wise believe.   49 The nobleman saith*
> *unto him, Sir, come down ere my child die.   50 Jesus saith*
> *unto him, Go thy way; thy son liveth.   The man believed*
> *the word that Jesus spake unto him, and he went his way.*
> *51 And as he was now going down, his servants met him,*
> *saying, that his son lived.   52 So he inquired of them the*
> *hour when he began to amend.   They said therefore unto*
> *him, Yesterday at the seventh hour the fever left him.*
> *53 So the father knew that it was at that hour in which*
> *Jesus said unto him, Thy son liveth: and himself believed,*
> *and his whole house.   54 This is again the second sign that*
> *Jesus did, having come out of Judæa into Galilee.*

The conditions which met Jesus as he returned to Galilee are summarized by quoting a proverb which he himself repeated on two subsequent occasions: "A prophet hath no honor in his own country."   For thirty years Jesus had lived among these Galileans, but they had not recognized him as a Prophet, they had no dream of his divine mission.   He had received no honor in his own country, but now he had been to Jerusalem and had become the center of interest: many had declared themselves ready to receive him as the Messiah for whom they looked, a political leader, a worker of miracles.   On his return to Galilee, his fame preceded him: "The Galilæans received him, having seen all the things that he did in Jerusalem."   They believed in him now because of his reputation and his works; but their faith was only incipient and imperfect, like that of multitudes in Jerusalem of whom we read that "Jesus did not trust himself unto them."   Incipient faith, however, might develop into perfect trust.   On the other hand, it might give place to doubt and hate.   In the sixth chapter of the Gospel we have an example of the latter; but here we have a charming instance of the former.

The picture of the nobleman of Capernaum illustrates the gradual development of belief. It is a miniature, but every feature is distinct, and the stages of the development of faith are as clearly drawn as in the case of the woman of Samaria, or of the man who was born blind. (Ch. 9.)

At first the nobleman's faith regards Jesus as merely a worker of miracles. He came to him because of dire need. He believed that Jesus could heal his son who was "at the point of death." He requested Jesus to come down with him to Capernaum and effect the cure. He received what may have seemed a severe rebuke: "Except ye see signs and wonders, ye will in no wise believe." In these words, however, our Lord was expressing the general attitude of the Galileans toward himself. Of this imperfect faith the nobleman was an example. The words of our Lord were intended to tell the nobleman of his need of a higher faith. They intimated that Christ claimed to be much more than a performer of wonders. He wished men to know and trust and commit themselves to him. There must have been much in the accents and the appearance of Christ to soften the apparent harshness of his reply. Surely the petitioner was not discouraged. There is only more of faith and intensity in his repeated request: "Sir, come down ere my child die."

Jesus now applies a severe test, yet one designed to instruct the petitioner and to develop his faith: "Go thy way; thy son liveth." It was difficult for the nobleman to leave the Prophet whom he had hoped to bring to his home. It was not easy to believe that his son had been cured so instantly. The command of the Lord indicated that he possessed more power than the man had supposed, and that he could heal at a distance, and out of the unseen. The nobleman's faith rises to meet this new demand; with no delay he leaves the Lord and starts for his home. He now believes not merely reports of the power of Christ; he is resting confidently upon the word of Christ. A third stage is reached as he meets his rejoicing servants and learns from them that the child not only had begun to improve, but had been cured, at the very hour when the Lord gave the promise of hope.   He is now ready to entrust himself to Christ, to confess his belief, and to bring all his household to a position of absolute trust and devotion.

The historian concludes the story by reminding us that this is the second of two miracles, each wrought at Cana of Galilee, and each marking a certain crisis in the career of our Lord.

What a strange contrast is at first suggested by the circumstances of these two "signs": the home of gladness and marriage festivity and the darkened home of anxiety and pain and the shadow of death!   However, both miracles contain testimony to the divine Person of Christ, both result in a deepening faith, both illustrate the joy and blessedness which result from trust in him.

Then, too, as the first miracle brought to a joyous close the private career of our Lord before he offered himself to the Jews as their predicted Messiah, so this second recorded sign ends the opening scenes of his public career, and reminds us that during the coming days of suspicion and hatred and opposition there are those, like this nobleman of Capernaum, who trust him and love him, and that too in the city which he has chosen for the time as his home.

2. THE FULLER MANIFESTATION   Chs. 5 to 11

The fifth chapter of John opens a distinct section in the narrative of the public ministry of our Lord.   Here while faith is seen to develop in certain individual cases, unbelief is almost universal and it deepens into anger and deadly hate.   A great conflict opens between Christ and the leaders of the Jews who finally determine to destroy him.   These seven chapters may be further divided as follows:

a. The "Sign" on the Sabbath; and the Beginning of the Conflict.   Chs. 5 to 8 b. The Sixth "Sign"; and the Formal Breach with the Religious Leaders. Chs. 9; 10

c. The Supreme "Sign"; and the Conspiracy of the Rulers. Ch. 11

It will thus be seen that each of these divisions begins with a miracle which is the occasion of increasing opposition and hatred, until at last the enemies of our Lord formally agree upon his death.

The first division is itself composed of three separate paragraphs:

(1) The "Sign" on the Sabbath; and the Outbreak of Hostility in Jerusalem. Ch. 5

(2) The Crisis of Belief in Galilee. Ch. 6

(3) The Continuation of the Conflict in Jerusalem. Chs. 7; 8

(1) The "Sign" on the Sabbath   Ch. 5

Jesus the Source of Life

The Sign and Its Sequel   Vs. 1-16

1 After these things there was a feast of the Jews; and Jesus went up to Jerusalem.

2 Now there is in Jerusalem by the sheep gate *a pool, which is called in Hebrew Bethesda, having five porches. 3 In these lay a multitude of them that were sick, blind, halt, withered. 5 And a certain man was there, who had been thirty and eight years in his infirmity. 6 When Jesus saw him lying, and knew that he had been now a long time* in that case, *he saith unto him, Wouldest thou be made whole? 7 The sick man answered him, Sir, I have no man, when the water is troubled, to put me into the pool: but while I am coming, another steppeth down before me. 8 Jesus saith unto him, Arise, take up thy bed and walk. 9 And straightway the man was made whole, and took up his bed and walked.*

Now it was the sabbath on that day. 10 So the Jews said unto him that was cured, It is the sabbath, and it is not law-

*ful for thee to take up thy bed.   11 But he answered them,
He that made me whole, the same said unto me, Take up
thy bed, and walk.   12 They asked him, Who is the man
that said unto thee, Take up thy bed, and walk? 13 But he
that was healed knew not who it was; for Jesus had conveyed himself away, a multitude being in the place.   14
Afterward Jesus findeth him in the temple, and said unto
him, Behold, thou art made whole: sin no more, lest a worse
thing befall thee.   15 The man went away, and told the
Jews that it was Jesus who had made him whole.   16 And
for this cause the Jews persecuted Jesus, because he did
these things on the sabbath.*

This miracle wrought by our Lord in Jerusalem is said
to have been performed at "a feast," but whether at Purim,
or Pentecost, or some other festival, it is impossible to
determine.

It is said to have been wrought at the pool of Bethesda
which was near the sheep market, or "gate."   The exact
location is not known.   Neither the precise time nor place
concerns us; what is of importance is the significance of
the sign and its relation to the public ministry of Christ.
The miracle bore witness to his divine Person, as the Giver
of life.   It was the occasion of claims which first aroused
the hatred of the Jews.   It indicated the results of faith in
him.

The scene at Bethesda is a striking picture of the suffering, the selfishness, the sin, of the world, with which is
contrasted the healing service and salvation of our Lord.
He alone is able to repair the waste of humanity and to
save the lost.   His is a ministry of redemption.   While
the entire chapter deals with witness to the Person of
Christ, and with the blessed issues of faith, one striking
feature of the record of the miracle is its account of the
development of faith.

There are three stages, suggested by the words of Christ:

(*a*) The question, "Wouldest thou be made whole?"   It
implies a rebuke.   The man has lost hope.   He does not

expect to be cured. It might not be true to say that he
did not wish to be cured. In the realm of spiritual infirmity, however, there are many who have no expectation of
being healed. They are painfully conscious of their weakness and sins, but they have no hope of recovery. Some
have no desire. They love sin. For them the life of holiness and purity has no attraction. They may be at Bethesda; they may be familiar with church and Sacraments;
but they have no more than the vaguest hope of ever being made whole.

The question, however, is more obviously an intimation
of hope. There must have been something in the accent
or gesture of our Lord, as well as in the startling question,
to indicate that he was able and willing to heal. Faith,
however feeble, must have been awakened. Every yearn-
ing of the soul for spiritual health should be interpreted
as a promise and inspiration of the divine Spirit.

(b) The command, "Arise, take up thy bed, and walk."
The first word, "arise," suggests the need of resolution and
immediate action. "Take up thy bed," reminds the one
who is to be healed that there must be no thought of re-
lapse, no provision for falling back into the old way of
living, no fear for the future, but confidence in Christ.
"Walk" declares the need of entering at once upon the experience of the new life which Christ imparts. There
must be an immediate confession of faith, and performance of Christian duty. The command of Christ is always
a promise; whatever he bids us do he will give us power to
perform. As Augustine said, "Give what thou command-
est and command what thou wilt."

(c) The warning, "Sin no more, lest a worse thing befall thee." It might seem that such a caution was needless.
Thirty-eight years of suffering, brought on by sin, might
seem sufficient to keep a man from a further yielding to its
power. The sad truth is that no amount of suffering
brought on by sin makes one hate sin, however much he
agonizes over its results. The only safety lies in yielding

the will to the will of the Savior.

The man who was healed felt that he could safely obey the command of Christ in whom he had trusted for his cure. As he goes toward his home, bearing upon his shoulder the little mat on which he had been lying, the Jews rebuke him for thus working, and so desecrating the Sabbath. He replies that the one who healed him gave him the command he is obeying. We can argue that Christ, who gives us life and spiritual health, is a Lord, in obedience to whose will we shall find blessedness and joy. Even when opposed to social custom, or convention, or to the opinions of men, we must be true to him. He cannot fail to be the true Lawgiver, if he is the Giver of life.

The Claim   Vs. 17-29

17 But Jesus answered them, My Father worketh even until now, and I work.   18 For this cause therefore the Jews sought the more to kill him, because he not only brake the sabbath, but also called God his own Father, making himself equal with God.

19 Jesus therefore answered and said unto them, Verily, verily, I say unto you, The Son can do nothing of himself, but what he seeth the Father doing: for what things soever he doeth, these the Son also doeth in like manner.   20 For the Father loveth the Son, and showeth him all things that himself doeth: and greater works than these will he show him, that ye may marvel.   21 For as the Father raiseth the dead and giveth them life, even so the Son also giveth life to whom he will.   22 For neither doth the Father judge any man, but he hath given all judgment unto the Son; 23 that all may honor the Son, even as they honor the Father.   He that honoreth not the Son honoreth not the Father that sent him.   24 Verily, verily, I say unto you, He that heareth my word, and believeth him that sent me, hath eternal life, and cometh not into judgment, but hath passed out of death into life.   25 Verily, verily, I say unto you, The hour cometh, and now is, when the dead shall hear the voice of the Son of God; and they that hear shall live.

26 For as the Father hath life in himself, even so gave he to the Son also to have life in himself: 27 and he gave him authority to execute judgment, because he is a son of man. 28 Marvel not at this: for the hour cometh, in which all that are in the tombs shall hear his voice, 29 and shall come forth; they that have done good, unto the resurrection of life; and they that have done evil, unto the resurrection of judgment.

The man who had been cured argued that if Jesus had power to heal he must have the right to command, and could safely be obeyed.

The Jews argued differently. They concluded that one who acted contrary to their narrow interpretations of the law, must be a sinner. They began to persecute Jesus. Their opposition, however, gave the occasion for him to make the most startling claim that had fallen from his lips. Its full significance, as recorded by John, is clearly stated: "My Father worketh even until now, and I work." "For this cause therefore the Jews sought the more to kill him, because he not only brake the sabbath, but also called God his own Father, making himself equal with God." It is not sufficient to say that Jesus was claiming merely to imitate the beneficent work of God; he was asserting that his work was identical with that of God, and that he sustained an absolutely unique relation to God, whom he declared to be "his own Father." No wonder the Jews attempted to kill him. Either Jesus was a blasphemer and a deceiver, or else he was the Son of God.

The divine activity which Jesus claimed to share with the Father was twofold, and neither function could be performed by man. He was, as illustrated by his miracle, the Giver of life, and he was the Judge of mankind. This activity was in each case both present and future. He was, even then, the Source of spiritual life and renewal. He alone could heal the morally impotent. He could raise the soul from spiritual death; but the hour was coming when he would raise from the grave those who were under the power of physical death.   So, too, this judgment, like the power of resurrection, includes both "the present judgment for which Jesus said he was come into the world, and which men pass on themselves by the very fact of their attitude toward him, and his gospel, and also the future final judgment which manifests character and determines destiny."   Jesus therefore refers to two resurrections: a spiritual resurrection in which all believers in him are now, in this present age, rising to new life (vs. 24-25); and a bodily resurrection, which is still future; but of both he is the Author and Agent.   Could any man, save the divine Son of God, make such a claim as this, stating that "the hour cometh, in which all that are in the tombs shall hear his voice, and shall come forth; they that have done good, unto the resurrection of life; and they that have done evil, unto the resurrection of judgment" (vs. 28-29).

The Witness   Vs. 30-47

30 I can of myself do nothing: as I hear, I judge: and my judgment is righteous; because I seek not mine own will, but the will of him that sent me.   31 If I bear witness of myself, my witness is not true.   32 It is another that beareth witness of me; and I know that the witness which he witnesseth of me is true.   33 Ye have sent unto John, and he hath borne witness unto the truth.   34 But the witness which I receive is not from man: howbeit I say these things, that ye may be saved.   35 He was the lamp that burneth and shineth; and ye were willing to rejoice for a season in his light.   36 But the witness which I have is greater than that *of John; for the works which the Father hath given me to accomplish, the very works that I do, bear witness of me, that the Father hath sent me.   37 And the Father that sent me, he hath borne witness of me.   Ye have neither heard his voice at any time, nor seen his form.   38 And ye have not his word abiding in you: for whom he sent, him ye believe not.   39 Ye search the scriptures, because ye think that in them ye have eternal life; and these are they which bear witness of me; 40 and ye will not come to me, that ye may have life. 41 I receive not glory from men. 42 But I know you, that ye have not the love of God in yourselves. 43 I am come in my Father's name, and ye receive me not: if another shall come in his own name, him ye will receive. 44 How can ye believe, who receive glory one of another, and the glory that* cometh *from the only God ye seek not? 45 Think not that I will accuse you to the Father: there is one that accuseth you,* even *Moses, on whom ye have set your hope. 46 For if ye believed Moses, ye would believe me; for he wrote of me. 47 But if ye believe not his writings, how shall ye believe my words?*

Jesus now declares the testimony by which so great a claim is supported. It was not the testimony of man, but of God himself. Of course human testimony had been given. John the Baptist had been like a burning and a shining "lamp" and "for a season" the Jews had rejoiced in "his light." The great prophet had witnessed to this very oneness with God which Jesus had just claimed: "Behold, the Lamb of God!" and "This is the Son of God."

However, our Lord states that he has greater witness than the witness of any man. It is the witness of his Father, who is testifying to the divine Sonship of Jesus through the miracles which he is performing. The Father has, also, additional and equally important testimony. It is in the writings of the Old Testament Scriptures. They testified of the Son. Men did well to expect through a knowledge of these Scriptures to find life; but this life could be found only as they saw Christ revealed and yielded themselves to him, the real Source and Author of life.

Our Lord concludes his discourse by condemning the Jews for rejecting him. They claimed to believe the Scriptures; and they felt that in their rejection of Jesus they were loyal to Moses; Jesus declares that real loyalty to Moses would have led them to accept him, because, in the Scriptures, Moses had testified of him. He insists that the reason for Jewish unbelief is not lack of evidence but lack of love toward God. They were seeking glory from men, and this blinded them to the real truth concerning the Son of God. Thus, according to John, there is always a moral element in faith and unbelief. Where the heart is turned toward God in love and devotion there is awakened a repose to the testimony concerning his Son; faith results, and through faith the life eternal which the Son alone can impart.

Thus, too, the key to the Scriptures is their testimony concerning Christ, and faith in him transmutes truth into life.

(2) The Crisis of Belief in Galilee   Ch. 6
Jesus the Bread of Life

The transition to this chapter is apparently abrupt. In the last chapter we were in Jerusalem; in the next we shall be again in the holy city; but here we find ourselves in Galilee, and by the sea of Tiberias. There is, however, a real continuity of thought. In the last scene was depicted the hatred aroused against Jesus because he had healed a man on the Sabbath; he cannot with safety remain in Jerusalem; he therefore withdraws to Galilee; and now he is tarrying there, even though the feast of the Passover is being celebrated. In other words, John is indicating here the long Galilean ministry which is detailed by the other Gospels and is intimating that its origin can be found in the conflict which he has pictured as arising between Jesus and the religious leaders of the Jews.

Why, however, does John select, from among the many miracles of our Lord wrought in Galilee, the feeding of the five thousand and the walking upon the sea? It is because these miracles, with their related discourses, led to a crisis among the followers of Christ, resulting in a marked division and in an open confession of unbelief and faith. Chapter six is therefore both a proper sequence and a parallel to chapter five. The chapter contains three natural divisions: (*a*) The Miracles (vs. 1-21); (*b*) The Discourse (vs. 22-59); (*c*) The Crisis of Belief (vs. 60-71). The "discourse" may be properly separated into four distinct dialogues: That of vs. 25-40 results from a question by the Jews; the second (vs. 41-51), from murmurs of the Jews; the third (vs. 52-59), from a dispute among the Jews; and the fourth (vs. 60-65), from the decision to turn away from Christ. It may well be treated, however, as one sermon or discourse, because of its obvious unity of theme.

Feeding the Multitude   Vs. 1-15

1 After these things Jesus went away to the other side of the sea of Galilee, which is the sea *of Tiberias. 2 And a great multitude followed him, because they beheld the signs which he did on them that were sick. 3 And Jesus went up into the mountain, and there he sat with his disciples. 4 Now the passover, the feast of the Jews, was at hand. 5 Jesus therefore lifting up his eyes, and seeing that a great multitude cometh unto him, saith unto Philip, Whence are we to buy bread, that these may eat? 6 And this he said to prove him: for he himself knew what he would do. 7 Philip answered him, Two hundred shillings' worth of bread is not sufficient for them, that every one may take a little. 8 One of his disciples, Andrew, Simon Peter's brother, saith unto him, 9 There is a lad here, who hath five barley loaves, and two fishes: but what are these among so many? 10 Jesus said, Make the people sit down. Now there was much grass in the place. So the men sat down, in number about five thousand. 11 Jesus therefore took the loaves; and having given thanks, he distributed to them that were set down; likewise also of the fishes as much as they would. 12 And when they were filled, he saith unto his disciples, Gather up the broken pieces which remain over, that nothing be lost. 13 So they gathered them up, and filled twelve baskets with broken pieces from the five barley loaves, which remained over unto them that had eaten. 14 When therefore the people saw the sign which he did, they said, This is of a truth the prophet that cometh into the world.*

15 Jesus therefore perceiving that they were about to come and take him by force, to make him king, withdrew again into the mountain himself alone.

The feeding of the five thousand, together with the miracle which follows, is found in all four of the Gospels; the other miracles recorded by John are peculiar to his narrative. These are evidently selected for reasons stated above and also because so well adapted to further the purpose of the writer, which is to prove that Jesus is the Son of God. The first is a true act of creation. Five barley loaves and two small fishes are so multiplied by the power of Christ that they satisfy the hunger of a fainting multitude. Yet the miracle is a proof not only of divine power but of divine grace. It is the character and motive of the works of Jesus which constitute them "signs" of deity. Here is an act of compassion and love. Jesus has withdrawn across the sea for rest; the multitude follow him, and throng him. He feels no resentment, only pity for them, and joy that he can give them relief. He addresses the disciples and receives a statement of their confessed helplessness. He accepts from a lad his small store of provisions, and with it feeds the throng. Even the fragments remaining are sufficient for the needs of the disciples for days to come, and they are, moreover, memorials of the Master's divine act.

The effect upon the multitude was so great that they were ready to crown him king. Faith in Jesus seemed to have reached its climax; it was, however, not genuine faith; it was the belief in him as a Worker of miracles which had been aroused in Judea; by it the multitudes were led to expect a series of prodigies which would relieve physical and social distress and secure for them political independence. This faith was to be tested the following day, and to be found untrue. But Jesus is not now deceived. He quiets and dismisses the excited crowds; he sends his disciples across the sea, away from their dangerous influence; and, all alone, he departs to the mountain solitude to pray.

Walking on the Sea   Vs. 16-21

16 And when evening came, his disciples went down unto the sea; 17 and they entered into a boat, and were going over the sea unto Capernaum. And it was now dark, and Jesus had not yet come to them. 18 And the sea was rising by reason of a great wind that blew. 19 When therefore they had rowed about five and twenty or thirty furlongs, they behold Jesus walking on the sea, and drawing nigh unto the boat: and they were afraid. 20 But he saith unto them, It is I; be not afraid. 21 They were willing therefore to receive him into the boat: and straightway the boat was at the land whither they were going.

The walking on the water is a miracle which offers a striking contrast to the conception of Jesus which the multitudes had shown. It reveals, not a political leader, with power in a restricted, earthly sphere, but a divine Creator who has supreme authority in the universe. To the disciples, in the darkness and tempest, Jesus suddenly appears, walking on the sea. He does not suspend the law of gravitation, but shows himself superior to natural forces and independent of space. He enters the ship, and instantly it has reached the desired haven.

So is Christ ever with his followers in the midnight and the storm. Thus can he cheer and save. This very experience has been interpreted as a foretaste of the distress of his disciples when he is taken from them to die, and of their joy at the reunion with their risen Lord.

This incident is also thought to teach that those who truly trust Christ will find loneliness and opposition and tempests, but also the safety and gladness of a divine fellowship. Another symbolic interpretation draws a parallel between the picture of Jesus as he prays alone upon the mountain and then appears to rescue the disciples, and the prediction that the divine Savior, who is now interceding for us on high, will someday reappear to bring blessedness to his followers and peace to the storm-tossed nations of the world.

The Discourse   Vs. 22-59

22 On the morrow the multitude that stood on the other side of the sea saw that there was no other boat there, save one, and that Jesus entered not with his disciples into the boat, but that his disciples went away alone 23 (howbeit there came boats from Tiberias nigh unto the place where they ate the bread after the Lord had given thanks): 24 when the multitude therefore saw that Jesus was not there, neither his disciples, they themselves got into the boats, and came to Capernaum, seeking Jesus. 25 And when they found him on the other side of the sea, they said unto him, Rabbi, when camest thou hither? 26 Jesus answered them and said, Verily, verily, I say unto you, Ye seek me, not because ye saw signs, but because ye ate of the loaves, and were filled. 27 Work not for the food which perisheth, but for the food which abideth unto eternal life, which the Son of man shall give unto you: for him the Father, even God, hath sealed. 28 They said therefore unto him, What must we do, that we may work the works of God? 29 Jesus answered and said unto them, This is the work of God, that ye believe on him whom he hath sent. 30 They said therefore unto him, What then doest thou for a sign, that we may see, and believe thee? what workest thou? 31 Our fathers ate the manna in the wilderness; as it is written, He gave them bread out of heaven to eat. 32 Jesus therefore said unto them, Verily, verily, I say unto you, It was not Moses that gave you the bread out of heaven; but my Father giveth you the true bread out of heaven. 33 For the bread of God is that which cometh down out of heaven, and giveth life unto the world. 34 They said therefore unto him, Lord, evermore give us this bread. 35 Jesus said unto them, I am the bread of life: he that cometh to me shall not hunger, and he that believeth on me shall never thirst. 36 But I said unto you, that ye have seen me, and yet believe not. *37 All that which the Father giveth me shall come unto me; and him that cometh to me I will in no wise cast out. 38 For I am come down from heaven, not to do mine own will, but the will of him that sent me. 39 And this is the will of him that sent me, that of all that which he hath given me I should lose nothing, but should raise it up at the last day. 40 For this is the will of my Father, that every one that beholdeth the Son, and believeth on him, should have eternal life; and I will raise him up at the last day.*

41 The Jews therefore murmured concerning him, because he said, I am the bread which came down out of heaven. 42 And they said, Is not this Jesus, the son of Joseph, whose father and mother we know? how doth he now say, I am come down out of heaven? 43 Jesus answered and said unto them, Murmur not among yourselves. 44 No man can come to me, except the Father that sent me draw him: and I will raise him up in the last day. 45 It is written in the prophets, And they shall all be taught of God. Every one that hath heard from the Father, and hath learned, cometh unto me. 46 Not that any man hath seen the Father, save he that is from God, he hath seen the Father. 47 Verily, verily, I say unto you, He that believeth hath eternal life. 48 I am the bread of life. 49 Your fathers ate the manna in the wilderness, and they died. 50 This is the bread which cometh down out of heaven, that a man may eat thereof, and not die. 51 I am the living bread which came down out of heaven: if any man eat of this bread, he shall live for ever: yea and the bread which I will give is my flesh, for the life of the world.

52 The Jews therefore strove one with another, saying, How can this man give us his flesh to eat? 53 Jesus therefore said unto them, Verily, verily, I say unto you, Except ye eat the flesh of the Son of man and drink his blood, ye have not life in yourselves. 54 He that eateth my flesh and drinketh my blood hath eternal life; and I will raise him up at the last day. 55 For my flesh is meat indeed, and my blood is drink indeed. 56 He that eateth my flesh and drinketh my blood abideth in me, and I in him. 57 As the living Father sent me, and I live because of the

Father; so he that eateth me, he also shall live because of me. 58 This is the bread which came down out of heaven: not as the fathers ate, and died; he that eateth this bread shall live for ever. 59 These things said he in the synagogue, as he taught in Capernaum.

The discourse, delivered in the synagogue at Capernaum, gives the true interpretation of the miracle wrought for the relief of the multitudes. The lessons which Jesus draws remind us that all of his miracles were acted parables; in addition to their immediate purpose of grace and love, they contained divine messages of spiritual truth. Possibly the very essence of the discourse is contained in the words: "I am the bread of life: he that cometh to me shall not hunger, and he that believeth on me shall never thirst." (V. 35.) It is to be remembered that while the miracle gave the occasion and the background of the discourse, its immediate reference is to the request of the people for a "sign," such as the manna which Moses gave. The reply of Jesus is that he is himself the true Bread from heaven. He has come down from God; he is the true Manna, given for the life of the world. His body is to be broken, his blood shed; yet he is to ascend again to heaven. To all who put their trust in him he will give present satisfaction, future resurrection, eternal life.

Throughout the discourse, as in the previous chapter, testimony is borne to the divine Person of Christ; yet, by way of contrast, the stress is here laid upon the necessity for faith in him, and the results of true belief and trust. The character of this faith in Christ is expressed in the strongest imaginable terms, as being a true eating of his flesh and a drinking of his blood, by which is meant a complete identification with him, and an absolute dependence upon him, as a crucified, risen, living, divine Lord.

Among the many lessons commonly drawn from this narrative a few may be mentioned.

(*a*) Our Lord regarded the spiritual as more important than the physical needs of men. He did graciously feed a multitude by the sea, but his real mission was to give his life for the salvation of the world. When referring to the miracle, he did not preach on labor, wages, and industrial conditions but on the need of spiritual life.

(b) Faith in Christ is promised to secure not merely healing but nourishment. In the previous miracle Jesus had given health to an impotent man; here he is sustaining the strong. It is not only the moral outcasts and lepers who need Christ, but the purest and noblest and best of men.

(c) Faith in Christ is not a luxury but a necessity. The people were given the simplest food, but they would have fainted without it. A Christian experience is not something which may or may not be added to other blessings of life. Without Christ there is no real life, here or hereafter.

(d) Faith centers in a Person. It is not the acceptance of a creed or the performance of a ritual, but consists in the surrender of self, in devotion and trust, to a personal, present, loving Savior.

(e) Faith is not compared with tasting, or admiring, but with eating. It has been declared to mean identification with Christ. He must be taken into every sphere and experience of life. His words and will must be assimilated, and become a part of our very being.

(f) Faith results in service; it is sharing, not keeping. Our knowledge of Christ is intended for the world. The disciples were given food to give to the multitude. Our talents may be few, our contributions consciously inadequate; let the Master bless them and their multiplied possibilities will serve thousands.

(g) Faith brings satisfaction, not mere temporary relief. It is not only the supply for a single meal, but the "twelve baskets full" that the true disciples find. Faith brings to them abiding, abounding, eternal life. The hungering, dissatisfied soul never turns to Christ in vain.

The Crisis of Unbelief   Vs. 60-71

60 Many therefore of his disciples, when they heard this, *said, This is a hard saying; who can hear it?   61 But Jesus knowing in himself that his disciples murmured at this, said unto them, Doth this cause you to stumble?   62* What *then if ye should behold the Son of man ascending where he was before?   63 It is the spirit that giveth life; the flesh profiteth nothing: the words that I have spoken unto you are spirit, and are life.   64 But there are some of you that believe not.   For Jesus knew from the beginning who they were that believed not, and who it was that should betray him.   65 And he said, For this cause have I said unto you, that no man can come unto me, except it be given unto him of the Father.*

66 Upon this many of his disciples went back, and walked no more with him.   67 Jesus said therefore unto the twelve, Would ye also go away?   68 Simon Peter answered him, Lord, to whom shall we go? thou hast the words of eternal life.   69 And we have believed and know that thou art the Holy One of God.   70 Jesus answered them, Did not I choose you the twelve, and one of you is a devil?   71 Now he spake of Judas the son *of Simon Iscariot, for he it was that should betray him,* being *one of the twelve.*

The crisis of unbelief may be suggested by the truth last stated, namely, that real faith in Christ results in an abiding satisfaction.   There were multitudes in whom the miracle had awakened wonder, and an incipient faith in Christ.   They had never trusted him, never been satisfied in him.   The word he is now speaking relative to the necessity of eating his flesh and drinking his blood seems to them difficult to understand.   They appear incapable of comprehending spiritual truth.

Our Lord intimates that their bewilderment will only be increased when he has withdrawn into the sphere of the unseen.   Those, however, who accept his words will find them the channel of new spiritual life.   Jesus is not surprised at unbelief among his followers; he knew there was a traitor even in the circle of his closest friends.

"Upon this many of his disciples went back, and walked no more with him." They were disappointed that he was not a political leader, they were unable to appreciate his spiritual teachings. There were some, however, who trusted him. "Jesus said therefore unto the twelve, Would ye also go away? Simon Peter answered him, Lord, to whom shall we go? thou hast the words of eternal life. And we have believed and know that thou art the Holy One of God." There are men today who are troubled by the truths concerning the divine Person and atoning death of Christ, and the need of faith in him. When these truths are pressed, they are ready to turn away. There are also those like Peter, however, who have believed the words of Christ, and have found in him such satisfaction of soul that they feel that there is none other to whom they can go, none other whom they desire. The claims of Christ are still tests of faith. They are still producing crises in the lives of his followers. They are dividing the false from the true. They cause many who have been nominal Christians to turn back from him; they give occasion to true believers to confess joyfully their satisfaction and their triumphant faith.

(3) The Continuation of the Conflict in Jerusalem
Chs. 7; 8

(a) The Witness at the Feast of Tabernacles   Ch. 7

Jesus the Riven Rock

Before the Feast   Vs. 1-13

1 And after these things Jesus walked in Galilee: for he would not walk in Judæa, because the Jews sought to kill him. 2 Now the feast of the Jews, the feast of tabernacles, was at hand. 3 His brethren therefore said unto him, Depart hence, and go into Judæa, that thy disciples also may behold thy works which thou doest. 4 For no man doeth anything in secret, and himself seeketh to be known openly.

If thou doest these things, manifest thyself to the world.
5 For even his brethren did not believe on him.   6 Jesus
therefore saith unto them, My time is not yet come; but
your time is always ready.   7 The world cannot hate you;
but me it hateth, because I testify of it, that its works are
evil.   8 Go ye up unto the feast: I go not up unto this
feast; because my time is not yet fulfilled.   9 And having
said these things unto them, he abode still *in Galilee.*

10 But when his brethren were gone up unto the feast,
then went he also up, not publicly, but as it were in secret.
11 The Jews therefore sought him at the feast, and said,
Where is he?   12 And there was much murmuring among
the multitudes concerning him: some said, He is a good
man; others said, Not so, but he leadeth the multitude
astray.   13 Yet no man spake openly of him for fear of
the Jews.

In weighing the evidence for the deity of Christ as presented by John, we should not fail to include the divine
knowledge of the future which our Lord was shown to
possess. He knew beforehand exactly the time and nature of his death, and frequently referred to the "hour"
which was to come. It is this fact which explains the
conversation between Jesus and his brothers, shortly before the Feast of Tabernacles. During the six months
following the Passover, when the crisis of unbelief had occurred, Jesus continued his ministry in Galilee. As another great national festival approached, his brothers
urged him to go to Jerusalem and to declare boldly and
publicly that he was the Messiah. They had no real faith
in him; but they wished to have his claims tested, and if
they were true, to have Jesus receive national recognition.
"Jesus therefore saith unto them, My time is not yet come;
but your time is always ready. The world cannot hate
you; but me it hateth, because I testify of it, that its works
are evil. . . . But when his brethren were gone up unto
the feast, then went he also up, not publicly, but as it
were in secret." There was no deception here, no incon-
sistency, not even a sudden change of mind. Jesus knew
that the time had not come for his final public manifesta-

tion to Israel. It was not at a Feast of Tabernacles that
he was to die, but at a Passover, as the paschal Lamb
who would take away the sin of the world. His earthly
ministry was not yet finished. He did not wish to precipi-
tate the crisis. The hour for the final tragedy and triumph
had not struck. This is what Jesus meant when he said
that his time was "not yet come." He would not go up
to the feast in the manner and for the purpose suggested
by his brethren. He went up "not publicly, but as it
were in secret."

There was a deep significance in the words, "Your time
is always ready." Jesus intimated that they were so far
in harmony with the spirit and practices of the world that
they had nothing to fear from the world, but he had in-
curred its hatred by his witness against its sin. Should
not the followers of Christ ask themselves the question
whether their aims and temper and conduct are more calculated to grieve their Master or to arouse the enmity of
an unbelieving world?

The brothers of Jesus, however, are not the only ones
who are concerned about his attendance at the feast. He
has become a character of national interest. His claims
cannot be disregarded. The rulers are watching for his
appearance, and the multitudes are divided in their opinions of him, some declaring him to be a "good man,"
others that "he leadeth the multitude astray." So men
today are compelled to face the claims of Christ. These
cannot be put aside. They sustain a vital and personal
relation to every immortal soul. There can be but two
possible judgments passed: Jesus was either a good man or
an impostor; but he could not have been "good" unless he
was the divine Son of God, for such he claimed to be.

During the Feast   Vs. 14-36

*14 But when it was now the midst of the feast Jesus
went up into the temple, and taught. 15 The Jews therefore marvelled, saying, How knoweth this man letters, hav-*

ing never learned? 16 Jesus therefore answered them, and said, My teaching is not mine, but his that sent me. 17 If any man willeth to do his will, he shall know of the teaching, whether it is of God, or whether I speak from myself. 18 He that speaketh from himself seeketh his own glory: but he that seeketh the glory of him that sent him, the same is true, and no unrighteousness is in him. 19 Did not Moses give you the law, and yet none of you doeth the law? Why seek ye to kill me? 20 The multitude answered, Thou hast a demon: who seeketh to kill thee? 21 Jesus answered and said unto them, I did one work, and ye all marvel because thereof. 22 Moses hath given you circumcision (not that it is of Moses, but of the fathers); and on the sabbath ye circumcise a man. 23 If a man receiveth circumcision on the sabbath, that the law of Moses may not be broken; are ye wroth with me, because I made a man every whit whole on the sabbath? 24 Judge not according to appearance, but judge righteous judgment.

25 Some therefore of them of Jerusalem said, Is not this he whom they seek to kill? 26 And lo, he speaketh openly, and they say nothing unto him. Can it be that the rulers indeed know that this is the Christ? 27 Howbeit we know this man whence he is: but when the Christ cometh, no one knoweth whence he is. 28 Jesus therefore cried in the temple, teaching and saying, Ye both know me, and know whence I am; and I am not come of myself, but he that sent me is true, whom ye know not. 29 I know him; because I am from him, and he sent me. 30 They sought therefore to take him: and no man laid his hand on him, because his hour was not yet come. 31 But of the multitude many believed on him; and they said, When the Christ shall come, will he do more signs than those which this man hath done? 32 The Pharisees heard the multitude murmuring these things concerning him; and the chief priests and the Pharisees sent officers to take him. 33 Jesus therefore said, Yet a little while am I with you, and I go unto him that sent me. 34 Ye shall seek me, and shall not find me: and where I am, ye cannot come. 35 The Jews therefore said among themselves, Whither will this man go that we shall not find him? will he go unto the Dispersion among the Greeks, and teach the Greeks? 36 What is this

*word that he said, Ye shall seek me, and shall not find me;
and where I am, ye cannot come?*

During the feast, Jesus appears and teaches publicly
in the Temple. He there intimates how serious a judgment
one who rejects his claims pronounces upon himself. The
rulers wonder at the depth of meaning which is being
drawn from the Scriptures by Jesus, a man who has never
attended their schools. He replies: "My teaching is not
mine, but his that sent me. If any man willeth to do his
will, he shall know of the teaching, whether it is of God,
or whether I speak from myself." That is to say, as his
teaching and claims are of divine origin they will be accepted as such by all who are in sympathy with the divine
will. Faith has more to do with the moral than the intellectual faculties; it is more a question of spiritual sympathy than of external evidence. One who is eager to do
the will of God cannot fail to yield himself to the Son of
God, when he has been clearly revealed in all his matchless holiness and grace.

Jesus proceeds to defend his conduct. The only charge
ever preferred against him has been that of breaking the
Sabbath, in his cure of the sick man at Bethesda. He replies by showing that the Mosaic legislation itself justifies
this reputed breach of the law. It allows to be performed, upon the Sabbath, a rite which is related to health
and symbolic of holiness; can it be wrong then that Jesus
"made a man every whit whole on the sabbath"? Jesus
warns the Jews against such foolish and superficial judgments; but it is to be noted that he here makes a specific
claim of sinlessness. Has any other man been able suc-
cessfully to defend such a claim, in the light of the de-
mands of the law of Moses, or in the court of conscience?
As the multitudes begin to question whether Jesus is really
the Messiah, they are puzzled by the fact that they know
his parents and home and early life, whereas the coming
of the Messiah was supposed by them to be shrouded in

mystery.   Jesus publicly and solemnly declares that the knowledge they possess is only superficial; his true origin is from God and from heaven, and thither he is soon to return; he is to go away, and they shall not be able to find him.   Little did they understand his words which seem so clear to us as we read them; but do they contain for us no serious message?

Is it not true that men reject Christ on some such trivial grounds, or because of some such superficial reasoning? They know this or that, and have conjectured some third thing; but what did Jesus really do and say, what was his life, what were his claims?   Is it not only "a little while," also, that we have opportunity to accept him; is the time not fleeting, and will there possibly be regrets and remorse, when he has gone, or the day is done, and we no longer have opportunity to receive and follow him?

The Last Day of the Feast   Vs. 37-52

37 Now on the last day, the great day *of the feast, Jesus stood and cried, saying, If any man thirst, let him come unto me and drink.   38 He that believeth on me, as the scripture hath said, from within him shall flow rivers of living water.   39 But this spake he of the Spirit, which they that believed on him were to receive: for the Spirit was not yet* given; *because Jesus was not yet glorified.   40* Some *of the multitude therefore, when they heard these words, said, This is of a truth the prophet.   41 Others said, This is the Christ.   But some said, What, doth the Christ come out of Galilee?   42 Hath not the scripture said that the Christ cometh of the seed of David, and from Bethlehem, the village where David was?   43 So there arose a division in the multitude because of him.   44 And some of them would have taken him; but no man laid hands on him.*

45   The officers therefore came to the chief priests and Pharisees; and they said unto them, Why did ye not bring him?   46 The officers answered, Never man so spake.   47 The Pharisees therefore answered them, Are ye also led astray?   48 Hath any of the rulers believed on him, or of the Pharisees? 49 But this multitude that knoweth not the law are accursed. 50 Nicodemus saith unto them (he that came to him before, being one of them), 51 Doth our law judge a man, except it first hear from himself and know what he doeth? 52 They answered and said unto him, Art thou also of Galilee? Search, and see that out of Galilee ariseth no prophet.

On the last day of the feast, Jesus made his supreme claim, and gave the climax of his teaching relative to the life which would result from faith in him.

He declared that he fulfilled in his own Person all the great realities symbolized by the feast, and that his followers would realize all typified blessedness and joy. Tabernacles commemorated the wilderness life of ancient Israel, and, as the harvest festival, celebrated also the goodness of God. The people dwelt in booths, and the chief rites of the eight days of the feast called to mind the miraculous blessings of Israel's pilgrim journey. Every morning a libation made in the Temple called to mind the water which Moses had brought forth from the riven rock. This libation was of water brought in a golden pitcher from the pool of Siloam and poured out in the Temple, amid the sounding of trumpets and the shouting of the rejoicing multitudes. It is quite probable that upon the last day of the feast, the eighth day, "the great day," this rite was omitted, either to suggest the blessedness of Israel when the people had entered the land of promise, or to indicate the thirst for the greater spiritual blessings of which the prophets had sung and which had not yet been realized. Surely Jesus saw in those multitudes, and in the weary throngs they represented, the countless souls which have been making their pilgrimages through all ages and lands, thirsting and fainting and distressed. They were in his mind when he stood and cried: "If any man thirst, let him come unto me and drink. He that believeth on me, as the scripture hath said, from within him shall flow rivers of living water." Jesus was claiming that he was to be for all the weary, unsatisfied, thirsty world, what the riven rock had been for Israel of old. No greater claim could be made, nor under more impressive circumstances. Yet Jesus adds a promise of the blessedness which would belong to his followers more marvelous than any which had hitherto fallen from his lips. Those who were satisfied by him would become themselves sources of spiritual blessing, channels of spiritual life. His truth, his grace, his saving power, would flow through them for the saving and satisfying of other souls. Their influence would not be meager and restricted, but like "rivers of living water."

The fulfillment of this promise would not be until Jesus had been "glorified" in death, resurrection, and ascension. Then, when he had been revealed in his true character as the divine Son of God, as the Savior of the world, then his Spirit would come in Pentecostal power upon all those who put their trust in him.

Such claims and promises were variously received. It is ever so. This is a chapter in which, as is always true in John, we read not only of testimony to the divine Person of Christ and of promises of new life to his followers, but of the development of faith and unbelief. The same testimony produces contrasted effects in different persons. The chapter opened with a statement of the unbelief of the men who for long years had been in the household of Jesus; and now we read that, after the matchless claim of Christ and his promise of "living water," there was a division in the multitude because of him. Yet the most striking contrast is that with which the chapter closes. Officers have been sent to arrest Jesus; they return to the council of rulers confessing that "Never man so spake." The Pharisees rebuke them in bitter scorn and assert that only hopeless ignorance can accept the claims of Jesus. One of their number however, Nicodemus, he that came to Jesus by night, declares that their law, for ignorance of which they are despising the common people, rebukes them for condemning Jesus without granting him a just hearing. His defense is weak and lacking in moral courage, but it springs from growing faith.

The multitudes always hear Christ willingly. Where there is no pride of intellect, there his words are welcomed, there his promises are gladly received. The enemies of Christ have usually acted without reason toward him, seldom allowing him fairly to present his claims; they have great knowledge of "law," and human wisdom, but do not honestly face his words and works. Nicodemus is facing the light; he is seeking for the truth; he is of a timid temperament; he will miss his truest joy; but we shall find him at last a disciple, bringing his hundredweight of spices to the tomb to show his devotion to the Lord he really loved.

(b) Jesus and the Sinful Woman   Chs. 7:53 to 8:11

53 [And they went every man unto his own house: 1 but Jesus went unto the mount of Olives. 2 And early in the morning he came again into the temple, and all the people came unto him; and he sat down, and taught them. 3 And the scribes and the Pharisees bring a woman taken in adultery; and having set her in the midst, 4 they say unto him, Teacher, this woman hath been taken in adultery, in the very act. 5 Now in the law Moses commanded us to stone such: what then sayest thou of her? 6 And this they said, trying him, that they might have whereof *to accuse him. But Jesus stooped down, and with his finger wrote on the ground. 7 But when they continued asking him, he lifted up himself, and said unto them, He that is without sin among you, let him first cast a stone at her. 8 And again he stooped down, and with his finger wrote on the ground. 9 And they, when they heard it, went out one by one, beginning from the eldest,* even *unto the last: and Jesus was left alone, and the woman, where she was, in the midst. 10 And Jesus lifted up himself, and said unto her, Woman, where are they? did no man condemn thee? 11 And she said, No man, Lord. And Jesus said, Neither do I condemn thee: go thy way; from henceforth sin no more.]*

This disputed passage is probably a true apostolic tradition introduced by some later editor of the Gospel, but it is so characterized by "the wisdom, holiness, and goodness of him to whom it is attributed, that it could no more have been invented than any other feature in the inimitable Life of Christ."

The motive of the Pharisees is not love for God, or zeal for righteousness, or a passion for purity and holiness, or indignation against sin, but wholly the desire to entangle Jesus and to secure from him some word or utterance which may lead to his arrest and condemnation and death. It is worthy of notice that the desire which men often feel for the punishment of offenders can be traced to motives which are discreditable, if they could be truly revealed. The religion of some men seems to consist in hatred of their fellows, or in a passion for the punishment of others.

The employment of such means as the Pharisees used to entrap Jesus is a pitiful reflection upon their character. That they should be willing to form a plot so distressing and repulsive shows that they were ready to stoop to any measure in order to accomplish their desired end. We find that the character of men is often revealed by the instruments which they employ to secure their purposes.

The aim of the Pharisees was to place Jesus in a dilemma. Should he acquit the woman, he would then oppose the law of Moses. (Lev. 20:10; Deut. 22:22-24.) Should he condemn the woman to death, he would then encroach upon the power and authority of the Roman state (John 18:28-31); for the Romans had taken from the Jews the power of inflicting capital punishment. The dilemma is similar to that suggested by the question as to whether or not it was right to give tribute to Caesar. In this particular case, the attempt was to make Christ act contrary to either the ecclesiastical or the civil law.

The reply of Jesus is a revelation of his divine wisdom and grace. At first he hesitates to speak. He stoops and writes upon the ground. Just what he wrote is merely a matter of conjecture. His hesitation may have been due

to the shame which he felt, not only for the woman but for
her accusers. //Some, on the other hand, have thought
that he wrote, as suggested by a verse from Jeremiah, the
word "apostate," intimating how far from God were the
very men who claimed to be acting in the place of God
and in his service. Others have thought that Jesus wrote
the words which he uttered: "He that is without sin among
you, let him first cast a stone." By this utterance, Jesus
lifted the question out of the sphere of mere legal techni-
calities into the realm of moral realities. He showed himself to be qualified to judge rightfully all men; he silenced
and convicted and condemned his enemies. If these Pharisees were to be self-appointed executors of divine Justice,
then they should be like God in the purity of their lives.
They may not have been guilty of the particular sin in
question, although possibly our Lord referred to the fact
that impure thoughts are sinful as well as impure deeds;
but they were guilty of sin. Jesus does not here call in
question the right of human governments to inflict penal-
ties upon offenders, but he teaches that men who wish to
assume for themselves the function of official judges must
themselves be pure. Evidently no one of that group felt
morally qualified, when tested by the standard Jesus pro-
posed. He thus upheld the law of Moses, but he convicted
the proud accusers of being themselves worthy of condemnation.

The defeat was most manifest; the Pharisees withdrew.//
They were led by the older men, who evidently had
formed the plan, and were followed by the younger, even
to the last. The fact that they did not take the woman to
the lawful judges suggests not only their defeat but the
malice of their design.

In the word of Jesus to the sinful woman he practically
made for himself a claim of sinlessness. He implied that
he could have pronounced the sentence which the Pharisees feared to pronounce; he could have condemned. He
did not pronounce the sentence, neither did he acquit the

woman of guilt. |He did not speak the word of pardon, for she had not come to him in penitence and in faith, as had the woman whose story is given in Luke 7:37-50. | He merely warned the woman, and gave her time to repent and believe. His word, however, was full of encouragement, and we cannot but conclude that she must have gone away to a new and better life.

His followers also have learned anew the lesson: "Judge not, that ye be not judged."

(c) The Crisis of Belief in Jerusalem   Ch. 8:12-59

The Claim and the Testimony

The Witness   Vs. 12-20

12 Again therefore Jesus spake unto them, saying, I am the light of the world: he that followeth me shall not walk in the darkness, but shall have the light of life. 13 The Pharisees therefore said unto him, Thou bearest witness of thyself; thy witness is not true. 14 Jesus answered and said unto them, Even if I bear witness of myself, my witness is true; for I know whence I came, and whither I go; but ye know not whence I come, or whither I go. 15 Ye judge after the flesh; I judge no man. 16 Yea and if I judge, my judgment is true; for I am not alone, but I and the Father that sent me. 17 Yea and in your law it is written, that the witness of two men is true. 18 I am he that beareth witness of myself, and the Father that sent me beareth witness of me. 19 They said therefore unto him, Where is thy Father? Jesus answered, Ye know neither me, nor my Father: if ye knew me, ye would know my Father also. 20 These words spake he in the treasury, as he taught in the temple: and no man took him; because his hour was not yet come.

Here Jesus compares himself with the cloud of glory which had led the Children of Israel through the wilderness. The memory of this cloud was brought to the minds of the Jews at the Feast of Tabernacles by the illumination of the Temple and of the city. Jesus had already compared himself with the riven rock; now he declares himself to be the true Pillar of fire. He claims that he is able to guide and to give light to his followers.

The foolish objection of the Pharisees is that in a law court it is necessary to have two witnesses, and that Jesus' witness is not true because he speaks of and for himself. Jesus replies that his Father bears testimony both by the written word and especially by the works which Jesus himself performs.

The Warning   Vs. 21-30

21 He said therefore again unto them, I go away, and ye shall seek me, and shall die in your sin: whither I go, ye cannot come. 22 The Jews therefore said, Will he kill himself, that he saith, Whither I go, ye cannot come? 23 And he said unto them, Ye are from beneath; I am from above: ye are of this world; I am not of this world. 24 I said therefore unto you, that ye shall die in your sins: for except ye believe that I am he, ye shall die in your sins. 25 They said therefore unto him, Who art thou? Jesus said unto them, Even that which I have also spoken unto you from the beginning. 26 I have many things to speak and to judge concerning you: howbeit he that sent me is true; and the things which I heard from him, these speak I unto the world. 27 They perceived not that he spake to them of the Father. 28 Jesus therefore said, When ye have lifted up the Son of man, then shall ye know that I am he, and that I do nothing of myself, but as the Father taught me, I speak these things. 29 And he that sent me is with me; he hath not left me alone; for I do always the things that are pleasing to him. 30 As he spake these things, many believed on him.

Jesus solemnly declares that if the Jews do not believe upon him they will die in their sins, that is to say, in the state of inward depravity in which death would overtake them and from which he might have delivered them.

Heaven will be closed against them, and only perdition can await them. Jesus further shows that sin is the alienation of the heart from God.

Moral Freedom and Divine Sonship   Vs. 31-59

31 Jesus therefore said to those Jews that had believed him, If ye abide in my word, then are ye truly my disciples; 32 and ye shall know the truth, and the truth shall make you free. 33 They answered unto him, We are Abraham's seed, and have never yet been in bondage to any man: how sayest thou, Ye shall be made free? 34 Jesus answered them, Verily, verily, I say unto you, Every one that committeth sin is the bondservant of sin. 35 And the bondservant abideth not in the house for ever: the son abideth for ever. 36 If therefore the Son shall make you free, ye shall be free indeed. 37 I know that ye are Abraham's seed; yet ye seek to kill me, because my word hath not free course in you. 38 I speak the things which I have seen with my Father: and ye also do the things which ye heard from your father. 39 They answered and said unto him, Our father is Abraham. Jesus saith unto them, If ye were Abraham's children, ye would do the works of Abraham. 40 But now ye seek to kill me, a man that hath told you the truth, which I heard from God: this did not Abraham. 41 Ye do the works of your father. They said unto him, We were not born of fornication; we have one Father, even God. 42 Jesus said unto them, If God were your Father, ye would love me: for I came forth and am come from God; for neither have I come of myself, but he sent me. 43 Why do ye not understand my speech? Even because ye cannot hear my word. 44 Ye are of your father the devil, and the lusts of your father it is your will to do. He was a murderer from the beginning, and standeth not in the truth, because there is no truth in him. When he speaketh a lie, he speaketh of his own: for he is a liar, and the father thereof. 45 But because I say the truth, ye believe me not. 46 Which of you convicteth me of sin? If I say truth, why do ye not believe me? 47 He that is of God heareth the words of God: for this cause ye hear them

*not, because ye are not of God. 48 The Jews answered
and said unto him, Say we not well that thou art a Samaritan, and hast a demon? 49 Jesus answered, I have not a
demon; but I honor my Father, and ye dishonor me. 50
But I seek not mine own glory: there is one that seeketh
and judgeth. 51 Verily, verily, I say unto you, If a man
keep my word, he shall never see death. 52 The Jews said
unto him, Now we know that thou hast a demon. Abraham died, and the prophets; and thou sayest, If a man
keep my word, he shall never taste of death. 53 Art thou
greater than our father Abraham, who died? and the prophets died: whom makest thou thyself? 54 Jesus answered,
If I glorify myself, my glory is nothing: it is my Father
that glorifieth me; of whom ye say, that he is your God;
55 and ye have not known him: but I know him; and if I
should say, I know him not, I shall be like unto you, a
liar: but I know him, and keep his word. 56 Your father
Abraham rejoiced to see my day; and he saw it, and was
glad. 57 The Jews therefore said unto him, Thou art not
yet fifty years old, and hast thou seen Abraham? 58
Jesus said unto them, Verily, verily, I say unto you, Before
Abraham was born, I am. 59 They took up stones therefore to cast at him: but Jesus hid himself, and went out of
the temple.*

To those who were his nominal followers Jesus now applies a test which will show whether or not their faith is
real. "Jesus therefore said to those Jews that had believed
him, If ye abide in my word, then are ye truly my disciples; and ye shall know the truth, and the truth shall
make you free." No passing emotion, no empty profes-
sion, constitutes Christian discipleship, but a patient continuance in the study and practice of the teaching and will
of Christ. The result will be a moral freedom not otherwise to be obtained.

His hearers are offended at the implication that they are
slaves. In spite of the political domination of Rome, their
consciousness of descent from Abraham, their consequent
hope of a national future in fulfillment of the promises,

their present enjoyment of social and personal freedom, all made them sensitive to any implication of servitude. Jesus reminds them that yielding to sin results in moral slavery but that faith in him as the Son of God will secure freedom from sin and the liberty of children of God. He insists that their claim to be children of Abraham is futile. Whatever the physical facts may be, they lack any real moral relationship to Abraham, as is evidenced by their deeds, and specially by their desire to kill Jesus.

If they were the true children of God, they would love and reverence the Son of God. Their hatred of him and failure to appreciate his message indicate that their actual moral relationship is with the devil. His activities are characterized by such enmity to truth and murderous hate as the Jews have been showing.

Thus Jesus again declares that faith and unbelief are less concerned with the mind than with the heart; they are due to moral states and sympathies. "If God were your Father, ye would love me. . . . He that is of God heareth the words of God."

Finally, Jesus makes a marvelous promise and a startling claim. "Verily, verily, I say unto you, If a man keep my word, he shall never see death." This is only a negative statement of the offer of eternal life which Jesus was again and again making to his followers. The blessedness of this experience would be a present possession, and the accident of physical death would not affect its essence; and in the resurrection of the body, this eternal life would reach its full fruition.

When the Jews interpret his words literally and object that death is a universal experience, Jesus startles them by replying that, for him, life has been, and ever will be, an eternal state: "Verily, verily, I say unto you, Before Abraham was born, I am." This is a claim of identity with God in his changeless Being. No wonder that the Jews "took up stones . . . to cast at him" as a blasphemer. Such he was, or else he spoke the truth. The claims of Jesus are unmistakable. He was either a deceiver or the divine Son of God.

b. The Sixth "Sign"; and the Formal Breach with the Religious Leaders   Chs. 9; 10

(1) Jesus and the Man Who Was Born Blind   Ch. 9

Jesus the Light of the World

1 And as he passed by, he saw a man blind from his birth. 2 And his disciples asked him, saying, Rabbi, who sinned, this man, or his parents, that he should be born blind? 3 Jesus answered, Neither did this man sin, nor his parents: but that the works of God should be made manifest in him. 4 We must work the works of him that sent me, while it is day: the night cometh, when no man can work. 5 When I am in the world, I am the light of the world. 6 When he had thus spoken, he spat on the ground, and made clay of the spittle, and anointed his eyes with the clay, 7 and said unto him, Go, wash in the pool of Siloam (which is by interpretation, Sent). He went away therefore, and washed, and came seeing. 8 The neighbors therefore, and they that saw him aforetime, that he was a beggar, said, Is not this he that sat and begged? 9 Others said, It is he: others said, No, but he is like him. He said, I am he. *10 They said therefore unto him, How then were thine eyes opened? 11 He answered, The man that is called Jesus made clay, and anointed mine eyes, and said unto me, Go to Siloam, and wash: so I went away and washed, and I received sight. 12 And they said unto him, Where is he? He saith, I know not.*

13 They bring to the Pharisees him that aforetime was blind. 14 Now it was the sabbath on the day when Jesus made the clay, and opened his eyes. 15 Again therefore the Pharisees also asked him how he received his sight. And he said unto them, He put clay upon mine eyes, and I washed, and I see. 16 Some therefore of the Pharisees said, This man is not from God, because he keepeth not the sabbath. But others said, How can a man that is a sinner do such signs? And there was a division among them.

17 They say therefore unto the blind man again, What sayest thou of him, in that he opened thine eyes? And he said, He is a prophet. 18 The Jews therefore did not believe concerning him, that he had been blind, and had received his sight, until they called the parents of him that had received his sight, 19 and asked them, saying, Is this your son, who ye say was born blind? how then doth he now see? 20 His parents answered and said, We know that this is our son, and that he was born blind: 21 but how he now seeth, we know not; or who opened his eyes, we know not: ask him; he is of age; he shall speak for himself. 22 These things said his parents, because they feared the Jews: for the Jews had agreed already, that if any man should confess him to be Christ, he should be put out of the synagogue. 23 Therefore said his parents, He is of age; ask him. 24 So they called a second time the man that was blind, and said unto him, Give glory to God: we know that this man is a sinner. 25 He therefore answered, Whether he is a sinner, I know not: one thing I know, that, whereas I was blind, now I see. 26 They said therefore unto him, What did he to thee? how opened he thine eyes? 27 He answered them, I told you even now, and ye did not hear; wherefore would ye hear it again? would ye also become his disciples? 28 And they reviled him, and said, Thou art his disciple; but we are disciples of Moses. 29 We know that God hath spoken unto Moses: but as for this man, we know not whence he is. 30 The man answered and said unto them, Why, herein is the marvel, that ye know not whence he is, and yet he opened mine eyes. 31 We know that God heareth not sinners: but if any man be a worshipper of God, and do his will, him he heareth. 32 Since the world began it was never heard that any one opened the eyes of a man born blind. 33 If this man were not from God, he could do nothing. 34 They answered and said unto him, Thou wast altogether born in sins, and dost thou teach us? And they cast him out.

35 Jesus heard that they had cast him out; and finding him, he said, Dost thou believe on the Son of God? 36 He answered and said, And who is he, Lord, that I may believe on him? 37 Jesus said unto him, Thou hast both seen him, and he it is that speaketh with thee. 38 And he

said, Lord, I believe. And he worshipped him. 39 And
Jesus said, For judgment came I into this world, that they
that see not may see; and that they that see may become
blind. 40 Those of the Pharisees who were with him heard
these things, and said unto him, Are we also blind? 41
Jesus said unto them, If ye were blind, ye would have no
sin: but now ye say, We see: your sin remaineth.

This story possesses an irresistible and unfailing charm.
A subtle humor pervades the dialogue between the Pharisees and the man who had been born blind; their ruffled
dignity and exasperation, and his irritating irony, are little
less than amusing, while against all stands the contrast of
the majestic calm of Jesus.

The witness to the divine nature of our Lord is of a
very unusual character. This is the best attested of all
his miracles. A public, official investigation of the alleged
cure was held, and as proof of its reality we have not only
the statements of the man, and of his parents and neighbors, but the unwilling admissions of the Pharisees themselves.

We also have here a significant example of the development of faith. The man born blind regards our Lord, at
first, as a man called Jesus, then as "a prophet," and finally as "the Son of God."

Most important of all, the miracle is an acted parable of
the life that issues from faith in Christ, the life of spiritual
illumination and moral vision, indicated by the great word
of the Master, "I am the light of the world." As the story
opens, Jesus and his disciples are arrested by the pitiful
picture of a beggar seated by the wayside, "a man blind
from his birth." The evident pity of the Master led the
disciples to propose the unsolved problem of the ages,
namely, the origin of human suffering: "Rabbi, who
sinned, this man, or his parents, that he should be born
blind?" They did not mean to imply that the man had
existed in a previous state, or had sinned before his birth.
They were assuming the universal law that sin brings suf-

fering, but were making the mistake of supposing that each individual case of suffering is due to specific sin; and they were puzzled to know how to apply their rule to the case of a man born blind.

"Jesus answered, Neither did this man sin, nor his parents: but that the works of God should be made manifest in him." He did not intend to teach that the persons in question were sinless, or that the man had been born blind for the sole purpose that he might be miraculously restored to sight. The statement is condensed. Our Lord does not attempt to explain the mystery of pain. He wishes to say to his disciples in all ages that the sight of human suffering should not suggest a theme for speculation but a call to service. It is not for us to question who has sinned; here is an opportunity for God to manifest his grace: "We must work the works of him that sent me, while it is day: the night cometh, when no man can work." Jesus is saying, and the message is for us, that the hours of life are few and limited, and there is a task for every hour; if we neglect our opportunity for service, it will be lost forever; night will come and our work will never be complete. The specific task for that hour was to open the eyes of the sufferer.

"When I am in the world, I am the light of the world." This clear claim of Jesus was likewise a promise. It must have aroused the attention of the blind man, possibly his hope. It was larger, however, than the limits of the present demand. To Jesus, the blind man was a picture of "the world" in its moral poverty and spiritual blindness; and his word was a claim that he was to give light and vision to all who would trust in him. He was saying, too, that it was not his words and teachings which were to be the source of such blessing, but his divine Person: "I am the light." He was not merely "a prophet," he was the Messiah, the "Sent One of God," the Savior. This marvelous claim is further emphasized by his act. He places clay on the eyes of the blind man and bids him go to the pool of Siloam and wash. Why? John explains, "The pool of Siloam (which is by interpretation, Sent)." Jesus had continually declared that he himself had been sent of God, and he is now intimating that he alone could heal; that he fulfilled all the blessings which Siloam typified. Each day of the Feast of Tabernacles a libation had been brought from that pool, to suggest the gifts of God to his people. Jesus is now saying that as the waters of Siloam will wash the clay from the eyes of the blind man, so he, the true Siloam, the One sent of God, will take away his physical blindness, and also will restore spiritual sight to the world.

The blind man, in faith and hope, obeys the command; he "washed, and came seeing"; and now the whole city is stirred by the report of the great wonder that has been wrought. It was indeed a marvelous "sign" and would go far to persuade men to admit the claims of Jesus. This his enemies feared. At all costs they must prove that the miracle has not been wrought. This they attempt to do, but without success. The man who had been given sight is summoned into the presence of the Pharisees and carefully cross-examined. Then his parents are summoned and they testify to the identity of their son, to the fact that he was born blind, and that he now sees. A second time the man is called and is urged to confess that the reputed miracle is only a deception. This is what is meant by their words: "Give glory to God: we know that this man is a sinner." "He therefore answered, Whether he is a sinner, I know not: one thing I know, that, whereas I was blind, now I see." He does not mean that he has no opinion as to the character of Jesus; but he says that he is willing to leave the theological problems to their superior wisdom; he knows, however, what Jesus has done for him; and he intimates that they must form their opinion of Jesus in accordance with the fact of his cure.

The dilemma of the Pharisees and their mode of reasoning are amusingly or pitifully reproduced today by many reputed wise men who attempt to prove that Jesus is not the divine Son of God. The Pharisees argued that the miracle had not been performed because it was the Sabbath, and God could not have healed a man on the Sabbath and by so working have broken the law of rest. That the Sabbath had been broken was merely their interpretation of a law; and they were thus opposing a theory to a fact, and on the ground of a speculation were denying a reality.

So today, substituting for the religious formula of the Pharisees the scientific axiom of the skeptics and rationalists, men tell us that the supernatural cannot exist, that miracles do not occur, and that the reputed works of Jesus are therefore mere fables; he was not born of a virgin, never opened the eyes of the blind, and did not rise from the dead. These wise men have theories and so they reject facts.

The Pharisees were, however, in a dilemma; there stood the man; his sight was perfect; he had been born blind; Jesus had opened his eyes. They must either deny the facts or admit the divine nature of Jesus which the facts proved.

The skeptics of today are troubled by facts. For example, they deny the miracles but admit that Jesus was a supreme moral Teacher, and they praise him as a "good man." But he claimed to have opened the eyes of a blind man; he made his disciples believe that he walked on the sea; he pretended to rise from the dead. Surely all this was base deception, or else Jesus was the divine Son of God. The Pharisees could not disprove the fact of the miracle, but they denied that Jesus was "good"; we cannot admit that Jesus was "good" if we deny the fact of his miracles.

The Pharisees tried to escape from their dilemma by calling the man and asking him to repeat his story, hoping to entangle him in his report. How modern skeptics would like to prove discrepancies in the Gospel story!

The man sees their dilemma and asks, in bold irony, whether their eagerness for more information about Jesus is due to their desire to become his disciples. They revile him, and declare that they are disciples of Moses, and that as for Jesus they "know not whence he is."

They have been driven to the position of the agnostic. It is a cowardly position; it is due always to a lack of the moral courage which is willing to face facts; it never commands respect; and the man who had been blind heaps upon it the ridicule and contempt it deserves. He states his simple unanswerable argument that an impostor, a deceiver, a sinner, could never have done the work that Jesus had wrought: "If this man were not from God, he could do nothing." The works of Jesus prove that he could not have been false in his claims.

The Pharisees excommunicate the man whom they cannot answer. How often does abuse take the place of argument; and how frequently do men dismiss with apparent contempt facts and proofs which they cannot deny or refute!

Jesus finds the lonely outcast, and leads him into more perfect light, until, as the scene closes, we find the man worshiping Jesus as the Son of God. In painful contrast stand the Pharisees. Their greater privileges, their knowledge of the Scriptures, should have made them the first to believe. Their boasted wisdom and insight are their very condemnation and the aggravation of their guilt: "Now ye say, We see: your sin remaineth." So it often happens that humble minds which have no wisdom of their own are the first to admit the claims of Christ; but this is no excuse for the wise and learned. Their very intelligence, if linked with moral sympathy and childlike humility, would make them the most devoted and helpful followers of the Master.

How then can faith be developed; how can "they that see not . . . see"? By imitating the man born blind; listen to the words of promise which Christ has spoken; obey his commands however strange; have the courage to hold to your convictions in the face of reputed "wise men"; be willing to suffer for his sake; and your spiritual sight will be strengthened, light will be cast on life's mysteries, and you will find Jesus to be indeed "the light of the world."

(2) Jesus the True Shepherd   Ch. 10:1-21

The allegory which opens the tenth chapter of the Gospel is inseparably connected with the incident of the chapter which precedes. It is in fact a continuation of the discourse which our Lord had begun in the presence of the Pharisees and of the man who had been born blind. The purpose was, first, to rebuke the Pharisees for their treatment of the man to whom Jesus had given sight; secondly, to encourage the man in his faith and trust; and thirdly, to describe the loving, saving ministry of our Lord.

The allegory contains three related but distinct pictures. It does not consist of a complete parable (vs. 1-6) and then two paragraphs of interpretation (vs. 7-10 and 11-18), but rather of three scenes, in each of which the imagery is slightly altered and the application different.

As one commentator suggests, the first may be a scene in the early morning, when the sheep are being led out from the fold by the shepherd; the second, a scene at noontide when the sheep are free to enter the fold for safety, or to go out into the pasture for the satisfaction of hunger; the third, a scene at nightfall when the returning flocks may be in danger of wolves. The first contrasts the unlawful tyranny of the Pharisees with the divine appointment of Christ; the second contrasts the injurious influences of their power with his gift of satisfying and abundant life; the third contrasts their cruel or cowardly motives with his self-sacrificing love.

1 Verily, verily, I say unto you, He that entereth not by the door into the fold of the sheep, but climbeth up some other way, the same is a thief and a robber. 2 But he that entereth in by the door is the shepherd of the sheep. 3 To him the porter openeth; and the sheep hear his voice: and he calleth his own sheep by name, and leadeth them out. 4 When he hath put forth all his own, he goeth before them, and the sheep follow him: for they know his voice. 5 And a stranger will they not follow, but will flee from him: for they know not the voice of strangers. 6 This parable spake Jesus unto them: but they understood not what things they were which he spake unto them.

Verses 1-6. In excommunicating the man who had been born blind, the Pharisees had given an example of their exercise of self-assumed authority. They were unauthorized rulers; Christ was the Messiah. The true people of God were dissatisfied with the Jewish leaders, and, like the man born blind, were ready to follow Jesus.

All this our Lord illustrated by his allegory. The Pharisees had not secured their power by entering "the door" of any divinely instituted office or function. They had climbed up "some other way." Their despotic power had been secured by illegitimate means. They were like thieves in their deceit and hypocrisy, and like robbers in their violence and audacity. Christ, on the contrary, had come on a divine mission, and in the appointed office of Messiah. He was the true Shepherd. John the Baptist, or others who had filled the prophetic office, like the porter at the door of the fold, had given him access to the flocks; and, as sheep recognize the voice of their shepherd, so, like the man whom Christ had healed, those who truly love God would gladly accept Christ as the Messiah. Our Lord even then intimated that to follow him would mean to separate from the Jewish state and synagogue and rulers, and to feel the loneliness the man had experienced who was unwilling to submit to the Pharisees; but he further indicates that a new flock is being formed, composed of his followers and enjoying the blessings of his guidance and care.

7 Jesus therefore said unto them again, Verily, verily, I say unto you, I am the door of the sheep. 8 All that came before me are thieves and robbers: but the sheep did not hear them. 9 I am the door; by me if any man enter in, he shall be saved, and shall go in and go out, and shall find pasture. 10 The thief cometh not, but that he may steal, and kill, and destroy: I came that they may have life, and may have it abundantly.

Verses 7-10. In this second picture, Christ is not the true Shepherd but "the door of the sheep." The way to divine communion and fellowship is through him. All others who have made such claims are "thieves and robbers." The influence of such is to "steal, and kill, and destroy," but those who come to God through Christ will have life abundantly; they will have true liberty and satisfaction and salvation.

11 I am the good shepherd: the good shepherd layeth down his life for the sheep. 12 He that is a hireling, and not a shepherd, whose own the sheep are not, beholdeth the wolf coming, and leaveth the sheep, and fleeth, and the wolf snatcheth them, and scattereth them: 13 he fleeth because he is a hireling, and careth not for the sheep. 14 I am the good shepherd; and I know mine own, and mine own know me, 15 even as the Father knoweth me, and I know the Father; and I lay down my life for the sheep. 16 And other sheep I have, which are not of this fold: them also I must bring, and they shall hear my voice; and they shall become one flock, one shepherd. 17 Therefore doth the Father love me, because I lay down my life, that I may take it again. 18 No one taketh it away from me, but I lay it down of myself. I have power to lay it down, and I have power to take it again. This commandment received I from my Father.

Verses 11-18. In this third picture, our Lord describes himself as the Good Shepherd, and declares that, as such, he is willing to lay down his life for the sheep. By way of contrast he refers to others who show that they are not worthy the name of shepherds, for their motive is selfish gain, and, in the face of peril, they show fear and cowardice. He calls them hirelings and declares that they flee when they behold "the wolf coming." As the Lord before designated the Pharisees "thieves and robbers" so here they must be related to the "hireling" and the "wolf." The latter pictures the cruel hate which animates his enemies; but there were among the chief rulers "many" who "believed on him; but . . . they did not confess it, lest they should be put out of the synagogue"; they were like hirelings; their real duty was to care for the sheep, but they were unwilling to make any sacrifice and therefore failed to protect Christ or his followers for fear of personal loss. However we may interpret the terms, "wolf" and "hireling," they stand in clear contrast with the Good Shepherd whose purpose is unselfish and whose motive is love.

Then, too, he has perfect knowledge of his sheep, and they know him; and this mutual relation is even compared with that which exists between Christ and his Father. This love and knowledge are not only for the disciples, who are represented by the man born blind, but also for a great multitude from among the Gentile nations who are to follow him. Christ declares that all who believe in him form one flock, although they may be in different folds. For all these he is to lay down his life. He is to die through the murderous hate of his enemies; yet his life is to be a voluntary offering for sinful men. However, he is to rise from the dead; this is his ultimate purpose, for only as risen, living, present, can he truly care for his sheep. Such power to live or die he has received from the Father, to whom his self-devotion is infinitely pleasing.

19 There arose a division again among the Jews because of these words. 20 And many of them said, He hath a demon, and is mad; why hear ye him? 21 Others said, These are not the sayings of one possessed with a demon. Can a demon open the eyes of the blind?

Verses 19-21.   The allegory is followed by this brief
historic note which describes the division among his
hearers that always resulted from the words of Christ.
It is characteristic of this Gospel, which ever deals with
the development of faith and unbelief, and shows that as
testimony is borne to Christ either by word or deed, men
are judging themselves by their response.   In the allegory, the testimony has been stated in the claims of Christ.
He has declared himself the Messiah, by presenting himself as the true Shepherd of Israel, the divinely appointed
Savior.   To these claims faith responded; the sheep heard
his voice.   By these claims unbelievers were angered: "He
hath a demon, and is mad; why hear ye him?"   In John,
however, in addition to testimony, and belief, there is a
third great idea: this is of the life in which faith issues.
Most beautifully is it set forth in this allegory.   In the first
picture its blessedness centers in the divine guidance
granted by the true Shepherd; in the second, it consists
in safety and liberty and spiritual satisfaction; in the third,
it includes the love of Christ, a knowledge of him, and fellowship of life, with all believers, of whatever fold or de-
nomination, in the one great flock of Christ.   Blessed indeed is he who can say from the heart, "The Lord is my
shepherd."

(3) Jesus the Christ, the Son of God   Ch. 10:22-42

*22 And it was the feast of the dedication at Jerusalem:
23 it was winter; and Jesus was walking in the temple in
Solomon's porch.   24 The Jews therefore came round
about him, and said unto him, How long dost thou hold
us in suspense?   If thou art the Christ, tell us plainly.
25 Jesus answered them, I told you, and ye believe not:
the works that I do in my Father's name, these bear witness of me.   26 But ye believe not, because ye are not of
my sheep.   27 My sheep hear my voice, and I know them,
and they follow me: 28 and I give unto them eternal life;
and they shall never perish, and no one shall snatch them*

*out of my hand. 29 My Father, who hath given them
unto me, is greater than all; and no one is able to snatch
them out of the Father's hand. 30 I and the Father are
one. 31 The Jews took up stones again to stone him.
32 Jesus answered them, Many good works have I showed
you from the Father; for which of those works do ye
stone me? 33 The Jews answered him, For a good work
we stone thee not, but for blasphemy; and because that
thou, being a man, makest thyself God. 34 Jesus answered
them, Is it not written in your law, I said, Ye are gods?
35 If he called them gods, unto whom the word of God
came (and the scripture cannot be broken), 36 say ye of
him, whom the Father sanctified and sent into the world,
Thou blasphemest; because I said, I am the Son of God?
37 If I do not the works of my Father, believe me not.
38 But if I do them, though ye believe not me, believe the
works: that ye may know and understand that the Father
is in me, and I in the Father. 39 They sought again to
take him: and he went forth out of their hand.*

*40 And he went away again beyond the Jordan into the
place where John was at the first baptizing; and there he
abode. 41 And many came unto him; and they said, John
indeed did no sign: but all things whatsoever John spake of
this man were true. 42 And many believed on him there.*

Two months have elapsed since the healing of the blind
man and the subsequent discourse at the Feast of Tabernacles. Jesus has been in Galilee, but he returns to Jerusalem to attend another national festival, "the feast of
the dedication," which celebrated the purification of the
Temple after its desecration by Antiochus.

Jesus is walking in an eastern cloister of the Temple
known as "Solomon's porch," seeking shelter from the cold
and rain of December. His enemies gather around him
in a circle and demand an explicit answer to the question
whether or not he is the Messiah. They are not sincere
in their request; they are well acquainted with his claims;
but they desire some occasion or excuse to destroy him.
Their question, moreover, is a difficult one; for he is not

the Messiah they are expecting, or such a Messiah as they are ready to receive; but he is the Messiah who has been predicted by the prophets, and who is to save those who trust in him.

Jesus replies with matchless wisdom. He declares that his miracles, wrought by divine power, are sufficient proof of the truth of his claims. He assures his questioners that their unbelief is not due to lack of evidence but to the imperfection of their moral disposition. If they were in sympathy with him and his Father, they would believe in him, and they would receive those supreme and eternal blessings, which he could impart. "My sheep hear my voice, . . . and I give unto them eternal life; and they shall never perish."

Jesus further states that this safety of his followers is due to the relationship which exists between him and the Father: "No one shall snatch them out of my hand . . . ; and no one is able to snatch them out of the Father's hand. I and the Father are one." This oneness means unity of will and of power, but it surely indicates even more, unity of being.

It was so interpreted by the Jews who at once "took up stones again to stone him," as they had done before when Jesus had claimed essential unity with God. They might have accepted Jesus as the Messiah, had he not made claims of deity. They did not expect a divine Messiah. It was because Jesus claimed to be one in essence with God that he was hated, rejected, crucified.

With indignant irony Jesus asks: "Many good works have I showed you from the Father; for which of those works do ye stone me?" The Jews answer: "For a good work we stone thee not, but for blasphemy; and because that thou, being a man, makest thyself God."

In replying, Jesus first frees himself from their charge, and then establishes the truth of his divine claim. (Vs. 34-38.) By his defense Jesus does not renounce his claim to deity; but he argues that if the judges, who represented

Jehovah in their appointed office, could be called "gods," in the Hebrew scriptures, it could not be blasphemy for him, who was the final and complete revelation of God, to call himself "the Son of God."

Jesus further replies that he was not only innocent of blasphemy; but, which is more important, that he has stated in reference to his Person only that which is true. His divine works of mercy and love are proofs of his oneness with God. If they will not believe his words, they should at least be convinced by these "signs."

The attempt to stone Jesus is for the time abandoned, and while his enemies are planning his arrest, he escapes from their hands, and withdraws from the city to a safe retreat east of the Jordan. Here, in the scene of the ministry of John the Baptist, many persons, influenced by the memory of the testimony of John and further by the miracles of Jesus, became his disciples. Their faith formed a striking contrast to the unbelief which had been reaching its climax in Jerusalem.

The breach between Jesus and the rulers is now complete, and it should be carefully noted that it was due to the claims of Christ to be, not only the Messiah, but the Son of God. This claim is here made with unparalleled clearness and defended by Christ on the ground of his miracles. To set forth such testimony was the first purpose of the writer of this Gospel. Whatever we may think of the Person of Christ, there can be no doubt that his enemies understood him to assert his essential and absolutely unique oneness with God; and he never intimated that they were mistaken.

Whatever view, too, we may take of the miracles, there can be no question that our Lord regarded them, and John records them, as sufficient evidence of his deity.

We should further consider what this section teaches as to the moral element in faith and unbelief. It is always a matter of the heart and will, quite as much as of the mind. Men do not believe because they do not desire to believe. The same testimony makes true disciples and deadly enemies. Christ is ever the Touchstone of character.

The third great feature of this Gospel should also be in mind, as we study these paragraphs; and we should observe what Jesus states of the life which issues from faith in him. He describes it in six striking phrases which set forth its blessedness in figures drawn from the very allegory with which this chapter opens.

The first two correspond to verses 1-6, and set forth the faith of the believer, and the personal interest of Christ: "My sheep hear my voice, and I know them." The second two correspond to verses 7-10, and intimate the faithfulness of the believer and the gracious gift of Christ: "And they follow me: and I give unto them eternal life." The last two correspond to verses 11-18, and suggest the safety of the believer, and the protecting power of Christ: "They shall never perish, and no one shall snatch them out of my hand."

Here, as throughout this Gospel, "eternal life" is a present possession of the believer, to be enjoyed and developed forever. Its main feature is not duration in time, but blessedness and heavenliness of character. It is the "abundant" life which Christ gives to all who put their trust in him.

c. The Supreme "Sign"; and the Conspiracy of the Rulers
Ch. 11

(1) The Raising of Lazarus   Ch. 11:1-44

This matchless narrative is of vital importance to the Gospel story as related by John. The miracle it records was the most marvelous and significant of all the "signs" wrought by our Lord; it awakened and strengthened faith in those by whom it was witnessed, while it aroused fear and deadly hatred in the rulers who now finally determined upon the death of Jesus; but, above all, it was a proof and prophecy of the life, present and eternal, which Christ imparts to all who put their trust in him.

Such a narrative needs little comment, and may be marred by any attempted analysis; yet it may be helpful to fix the thought successively upon some of its special features.

The Friendship   Vs. 1-6

1 Now a certain man was sick, Lazarus of Bethany, of the village of Mary and her sister Martha. 2 And it was that Mary who anointed the Lord with ointment, and wiped his feet with her hair, whose brother Lazarus was sick. 3 The sisters therefore sent unto him, saying, Lord, behold, he whom thou lovest is sick. 4 But when Jesus heard it, he said, This sickness is not unto death, but for the glory of God, that the Son of God may be glorified thereby. 5 Now Jesus loved Martha, and her sister, and Lazarus. 6 When therefore he heard that he was sick, he abode at that time two days in the place where he was.

What is here related of Martha and Mary and Lazarus reminds us of the friendships of Jesus. These were very real. The truth of the loneliness of our Lord may be overemphasized, except as we think of his isolation in the experience of atoning for sin. He possessed, however, a genius for friendship, he had his chosen companions, and there were homes where he was a welcome guest. "Now Jesus loved Martha, and her sister, and Lazarus." So, today, Christ has his inner circle of friends; they are not chosen arbitrarily, but they are composed of those who love him and respond to him and have the grace of hospitality in their hearts.

Of Mary and Martha we have the charming picture drawn by the Evangelist Luke, where the very love of Martha led her to assume such burdens that she became anxious and troubled and complaining, while the sensitive heart of Mary perceived that she could best entertain the Master by sitting at his feet and listening to his word.

But Mary also served: and her subsequent act of devotion had already become so well known that when John wrote this narrative he described her as "that Mary who anointed the Lord with ointment." This anointing is that which is related in the next chapter of this Gospel and is not to be identified with the story of the sinful woman related by Luke. Nor is Mary to be confused with Mary Magdalene. Mary of Bethany was the sister of Martha and Lazarus, in whose home Jesus loved to be.

Now trouble has come to this home. The friendship of Jesus does not protect us from human sorrows, but it gives us the assurance of sympathy and relief.

"The sisters therefore sent unto him, saying, Lord, behold, he whom thou lovest is sick." By his reply Jesus did not mean to say that Lazarus was not to die; nor yet that the purpose and sole explanation of the sickness was the opportunity for working a miracle of resurrection. He meant that the result of this sickness would not be the continued victory of death, but the manifested glory of God, in the triumph of resurrection and life. When distress comes to a Christian it is dangerous to assert that the purpose is some benefit, and that the explanation is found in some future blessing. The purposes of God are beyond our ken, and suffering is an unexplained mystery; but it is absolutely certain that, for a friend of Jesus, the result of suffering will be some eternal good, some manifestation of "the glory of God."

There are delays, however, by which our faith in the friendship of our Lord may be tried. "When . . . he heard that he was sick, he abode . . . two days in the place where he was." Jesus does not linger that Lazarus may die. He was already dead, and buried, before the message reached Jesus. The Lord came to Bethany on the fourth day (vs. 17, 39): one day was spent on his journey, one by the messenger on his, and two were spent by our Lord after the message of illness had come. He knew that Lazarus was dead; why he delayed we can only conjecture. The sisters had not asked him to come. They realized the peril involved in his return to Judea. When Lazarus died they sent no second messengers. Enough for them that the Master knew they were in trouble. They longed for him to come. They left everything to his decision. They were confident of his love.

Nor was such confidence misplaced. With the certainty that his action would result in the sacrifice of his own life, the friendship of Jesus brought him back to the home in Bethany. There are mysteries and delays in his dealings with us; but we need never doubt that One who gave his life for us has any other thought for us but love.

The Fearlessness   Vs. 7-16

7 Then after this he saith to the disciples, Let us go into Judæa again. 8 The disciples say unto him, Rabbi, the Jews were but now seeking to stone thee; and goest thou thither again? 9 Jesus answered, Are there not twelve hours in the day? If a man walk in the day, he stumbleth not, because he seeth the light of this world. 10 But if a man walk in the night, he stumbleth, because the light is not in him. 11 These things spake he: and after this he saith unto them, Our friend Lazarus is fallen asleep; but I go, that I may awake him out of sleep. 12 The disciples therefore said unto him, Lord, if he is fallen asleep, he will recover. 13 Now Jesus had spoken of his death: but they thought that he spake of taking rest in sleep. 14 Then Jesus therefore said unto them plainly, Lazarus is dead. 15 And I am glad for your sakes that I was not there, to the intent ye may believe; nevertheless let us go unto him. 16 Thomas therefore, who is called Didymus, said unto his fellow-disciples, Let us also go, that we may die with him.

We should note here the fearlessness of Jesus. "He saith to the disciples, Let us go into Judæa again." He does not say to Bethany, but to Judea, the place of peril. The disciples so understand his words and reply: "Rabbi, the Jews were but now seeking to stone thee; and goest thou thither again?" The reply of Jesus shows that his courage was due to a confident belief in the changeless purpose and providence of God: "Are there not twelve hours in the day? If a man walk in the day, he stumbleth not." He is asserting that he has been given a task to perform and time for its performance. No enemy, no accident, can shorten by a single hour the allotted day of his earthly life. The only peril would be in deserting the path of duty. That would result in darkness and loss. In the way of his appointed work he was absolutely safe.

Is not this true of each follower of Christ, and will not the acceptance of this truth concerning the task and time of life give us courage in seasons of peril and hardship and darkness?

Jesus then states clearly to his disciples the fact of the death of Lazarus, his purpose to raise him from the dead and his confidence that the miracle will strengthen the faith of his followers. They are still fearful, and Thomas is despondent, though faithful; but the intimation that he is to raise Lazarus from the dead, and the prospect of this wonderful work must have done much toward making them forget their fear. So as we follow our Lord in the path of duty, we are not only assured of safety, because he who allotted the task will also give the time and the strength, but we are cheered by the prospect of all that is to be achieved by his presence and power and grace.

The Promise   Vs. 17-27

17 So when Jesus came, he found that he had been in the tomb four days already. 18 Now Bethany was nigh unto Jerusalem, about fifteen furlongs off; 19 and many of the Jews had come to Martha and Mary, to console them concerning their brother. 20 Martha therefore, when she heard that Jesus was coming, went and met him: but Mary still sat in the house. 21 Martha therefore said unto Jesus, Lord, if thou hadst been here, my brother had not died.

22 And even now I know that, whatsoever thou shalt ask of God, God will give thee. 23 Jesus saith unto her, Thy brother shall rise again. 24 Martha saith unto him, I know that he shall rise again in the resurrection at the last day. 25 Jesus said unto her, I am the resurrection, and the life: he that believeth on me, though he die, yet shall he live; 26 and whosoever liveth and believeth on me shall never die. Believest thou this? 27 She saith unto him, Yea, Lord: I have believed that thou art the Christ, the Son of God, even *he that cometh into the world.*

The essential message of this entire narrative is embodied in the promise of Jesus: "I am the resurrection, and the life: he that believeth on me, though he die, yet shall he live; and whosoever liveth and believeth on me shall never die."

These marvelous words were spoken in reply to the request of Martha. She had heard that Jesus was coming. True to her nature she was the first to act, and while Mary still sat in the house, she went out to meet him. The words with which she greets him are not to be regarded as implying a complaint or a rebuke: "Lord, if thou hadst been here, my brother had not died." They express genuine regret, not that Jesus had delayed his coming after Lazarus had died, but that he had not been present during his illness, and kept him from death. Martha then adds what should be regarded as a request of triumphant faith; it did imply that Jesus might secure the return of her brother to life. Yet her faith was not perfect. It suggested that Jesus, as a man, might make a request of God, and further that the realm in which Christ was working was essentially physical and not spiritual. To develop her faith, Christ replies, "Thy brother shall rise again"; but the promise does not comfort Martha; she interprets it of a resurrection general and remote. "I know that he shall rise again in the resurrection at the last day," she answers. How truly does she express the feeling of countless mourners today! They are not satisfied, they should not be, with the assurance of reunions in the distant future. The heart craves something for the present, and needs a personal relationship with Christ. To Martha, and to every mourner, comes this incomparable promise of our Lord: "I am the resurrection, and the life." He does not need to ask that life shall be restored; he does not bid Martha to wait some future day; he is himself the Source of life-giving power. It is our relation to a present, divine Lord which gives us comfort. This spiritual fellowship is the basis and pledge of bodily resurrection and eternal reunion. "He that believeth on me, though he die, yet shall he live"; the body of the believer is certain to be raised; it is not to continue forever under the power of death. "And whosoever liveth and believeth on me shall never die." Faith in Christ is the source of a spiritual resurrection, which is a present and abiding experience of such blessedness that it cannot be affected by any bodily change. What is called death is but an incident in the course of an endless life. The believer never dies.

Can Martha accept such a marvelous revelation? Is she ready to believe so glorious a promise? "Believest thou this?" Her reply shows the strength of her faith and the clearness of her spiritual vision. Her hope is centered in the Person of her Lord. Her answer is voiced in words peculiarly characteristic of this Gospel: "I have believed that thou art the Christ, the Son of God." To trace the development of such faith is the purpose of the writer. That we may so believe, he is about to record a miracle which he relates as the supreme "sign."

The Sympathy   Vs. 28-37

28 And when she had said this, she went away, and called Mary her sister secretly, saying, The Teacher is here, and calleth thee. 29 And she, when she heard it, arose quickly, and went unto him. 30 (Now Jesus was not yet come into the village, but was still in the place where Martha met him.) 31 The Jews then who were with her in

the house, and were consoling her, when they saw Mary,
that she rose up quickly and went out, followed her, sup-
posing that she was going unto the tomb to weep there.
32 Mary therefore, when she came where Jesus was, and
saw him, fell down at his feet, saying unto him, Lord, if
thou hadst been here, my brother had not died. 33 When
Jesus therefore saw her weeping, and the Jews also weep-
ing who came with her, he groaned in the spirit, and was
troubled, 34 and said, Where have ye laid him? They say
unto him, Lord, come and see. 35 Jesus wept. 36 The
Jews therefore said, Behold how he loved him! 37 But
some of them said, Could not this man, who opened the
eyes of him that was blind, have caused that this man also
should not die?

In his meeting with Mary, our Lord specially reveals
his human sympathy. It has been manifested by his coming to Bethany, and by his words to Martha, but now it is
given an unrivaled expression. He sends to Mary a message, telling her of his presence and his personal desire to
see her; she hastens to meet him: she falls at his feet, expressing her faith in the words Martha has used, but voices
no request. Then, we read, "Jesus . . . groaned in the
spirit, and was troubled," and as he asked to be shown
the place of burial, "Jesus wept." It may be difficult to
determine exactly what is meant by groaning "in the
spirit"; probably, a deep indignation of soul at death and
all its suggestions of suffering and sin. Nor do we know
exactly the force of the expression: "He troubled himself";
probably, a physical shudder shook his body. When,
however, we read "Jesus wept," we can hardly misunder-
stand the words. Even though he knew that life was soon
to be restored, and joy to fill the hearts of those mourners,
the thought of the suffering that Lazarus had endured, and
of the present anguish of Mary, caused Jesus to express in
tears the sympathy of his loving soul.

In our time of bereavement, as we fall at the feet of the
Master, even though we believe in the miracle of the fu-

ture resurrection which will bring us our beloved again, we may be less in need of the instruction given to Martha than of the tender personal sympathy expressed for Mary by our Lord.

The Power   Vs. 38-44

38 Jesus therefore again groaning in himself cometh to the tomb. Now it was a cave, and a stone lay against it. 39 Jesus saith, Take ye away the stone. Martha, the sister of him that was dead, saith unto him, Lord, by this time the body decayeth; for he hath been dead four days. 40 Jesus saith unto her, Said I not unto thee, that, if thou believedst, thou shouldest see the glory of God? 41 So they took away the stone. And Jesus lifted up his eyes, and said, Father, I thank thee that thou heardest me. 42 And I knew that thou hearest me always: but because of the multitude that standeth around I said it, that they may believe that thou didst send me. 43 And when he had thus spoken, he cried with a loud voice, Lazarus, come forth. 44 He that was dead came forth, bound hand and foot with grave-clothes; and his face was bound about with a napkin. Jesus saith unto them, Loose him, and let him go.

It is not, however, to prove human sympathy but divine power, that this story is told by John; or possibly it is to show a divine sympathy which manifests itself in supernatural power. There is a matchless eloquence in these phrases of the narrative: "Jesus wept," "Lazarus, come forth"; here is love, linked with omnipotence.

In the record of the miracle we should note, incidentally, (*a*) the unbelief of the Jews, who were expecting no miracle; (*b*) the faith of Martha which needs a last word of encouragement; (*c*) the majestic confidence of our Lord, expressed in the prayer that the hearers might understand that they were to witness a work of God attesting the divine Person and mission of his Son.

Of the miracle itself it is to be observed that (*a*) it was an actual resurrection, such as cannot be explained as a case of mental healing, or on the ground of natural law; Lazarus had been dead four days. (*b*) It was unquestioned, even by hostile witnesses who were present in large numbers. (*c*) It was declared by our Lord, as no other "sign," to be wrought with the purpose of producing faith. Can a careful reading of the moving narrative leave, in a candid mind, any other conviction than that "Jesus is the Christ, the Son of God"? Shall we not, also, as we catch its deeper meanings, rejoice in the promise, which it gives to faith, of a life whose triumph robs death of its sting, and the grave of its victory?

(2) The Conspiracy of the Rulers   Ch. 11:45-57

45 Many therefore of the Jews, who came to Mary and beheld that which he did, believed on him. 46 But some of them went away to the Pharisees, and told them the things which Jesus had done.

47 The chief priests therefore and the Pharisees gathered a council, and said, What do we? for this man doeth many signs. 48 If we let him thus alone, all men will believe on him: and the Romans will come and take away both our place and our nation. 49 But a certain one of them, Caiaphas, being high priest that year, said unto them, Ye know nothing at all, 50 nor do ye take account that it is expedient for you that one man should die for the people, and that the whole nation perish not. 51 Now this he said not of himself: but being high priest that year, he prophesied that Jesus should die for the nation; 52 and not for the nation only, but that he might also gather together into one the children of God that are scattered abroad. 53 So from that day forth they took counsel that they might put him to death.

54 Jesus therefore walked no more openly among the Jews, but departed thence into the country near to the wilderness, into a city called Ephraim; and there he tarried with the disciples. 55 Now the passover of the Jews was at hand: and many went up to Jerusalem out of the country before the passover, to purify themselves. 56 They sought therefore for Jesus, and spake one with another, as they stood in the temple, What think ye? That he will not come to the feast? 57 Now the chief priests and the Pharisees had given commandment, that, if any man knew where he was, he should show it, that they might take him.

The chapter closes with this statement of the immediate results of the raising of Lazarus. As in the case of each "sign," the first effect was faith in Christ, on the part of those who had been witnesses of his power. The more serious result was the deepening of hatred in the hearts of the rulers and their determination to put Jesus to death. Their decision to take definite action against Jesus was due to the fear lest the continuance of such miracles might result in a popular uprising which the Roman Government would use as a reason or excuse for destroying the city and nation of the Jews. What gave final form to the deliberations was the unconscious prophecy of the high priest, Caiaphas: "It is expedient for you that one man should die for the people, and that the whole nation perish not." All that he meant to say was that, in utter disregard for right or justice, it would be better to murder Jesus than to allow their "place" and "nation" to be in danger; his motive was selfish, his counsel diabolical; yet his words contained a meaning of which he never dreamed. It was true that Jesus was to "die for the people," and to be the true Sacrifice for sin, and the Source of life, for those who put their trust in him. "And not for the nation only": the result of his death would be the formation of a new nation, even his church, in which would be gathered the children of God from among all the nations of the world. The unconscious prophecy is being fulfilled, but quite contrary to the thought of Caiaphas. The result of the death of Jesus was the destruction by the Romans of the very state Caiaphas wished to save, and the securing through Jesus of universal blessings of which Caiaphas never dreamed. No credit can be given to Caiaphas, and there is no excuse for his words; the latter resulted in the most cruel conspiracy the world has ever seen. "They took counsel that they might put him to death." Jesus withdrew for safety to a place of secrecy, until the hour of divine appointment, the true Passover season, should arrive. Then, while the multitudes speculate as to whether Jesus will appear in public, the rulers take further action that "if any man knew where he was, he should show it, that they might take him," to put him to death.

3. The Close of the Ministry   Ch. 12

The twelfth chapter of John contains an account of the last days of the public ministry of our Lord. In the five chapters which follow, or until the narrative of his Passion, he is alone with his disciples, revealing himself to them in secret.

The thought of the chapter moves in the sphere of the three dominating truths of the Gospel, namely, testimony that Jesus is the Christ, the Son of God, resultant faith and unbelief, and the life in which faith issues; but here special emphasis is placed upon the second of these features. Three incidents are sketched which depict, against a background of unbelief, the faith in Christ which his public ministry has developed; and the chapter closes with judgments, pronounced upon faith and unbelief, by John and by Jesus. The three incidents are (1) the anointing at Bethany, where Jesus is shown to be devotedly loved by his followers; (2) the triumphal entry into Jerusalem, where Jesus appears as the popular idol of the Jewish multitudes; (3) the last ministry in the Temple, where Jesus is the object of interest to the inquiring Greeks, who are typical representatives of the Gentile world. However, the discontent of Judas depicted in the first scene, the anger of the rulers in the second, and the reply of Jesus in the third, all prepare us for the coming tragedy of unbelief; so that this chapter serves to close the story of our Lord's ministry and to introduce the narrative of his death;

and its concluding words, from the pen of John and the lips of Jesus, summarize the results of the ministry of Christ, and the substance of his teachings.

a. The Manifestations of Faith   Ch. 12:1-36

(1) The Anointing at Bethany   Ch. 12:1-11

1 Jesus therefore six days before the passover came to Bethany, where Lazarus was, whom Jesus raised from the dead. 2 So they made him a supper there: and Martha served; but Lazarus was one of them that sat at meat with him. 3 Mary therefore took a pound of ointment of pure nard, very precious, and anointed the feet of Jesus, and wiped his feet with her hair: and the house was filled with the odor of the ointment. 4 But Judas Iscariot, one of his disciples, that should betray him, saith, 5 Why was not this ointment sold for three hundred shillings, and given to the poor? 6 Now this he said, not because he cared for the poor; but because he was a thief, and having the bag took away what was put therein. 7 Jesus therefore said, Suffer her to keep it against the day of my burying. 8 For the poor ye have always with you; but me ye have not always.

9 The common people therefore of the Jews learned that he was there: and they came, not for Jesus' sake only, but that they might see Lazarus also, whom he had raised from the dead. 10 But the chief priests took counsel that they might put Lazarus also to death; 11 because that by reason of him many of the Jews went away, and believed on Jesus.

The life of Mary is painted for us in three memorable pictures, in each of which she is found at the feet of Jesus. In the first she is seated at his feet listening to his word; in the second she has fallen at his feet, seeking sympathy and help; in the third she is anointing his feet to express her devoted love. It has been a cruel mistake on the part of some to identify her, as she appears in this last picture, either with Mary Magdalene or with the sinful woman who anointed the feet of Jesus with her tears. Here is the same pure, gentle, sensitive, loving friend who was

sketched for us entertaining the Lord in her home in
Bethany.   There she was contrasted with her sister
Martha; and it would be truly interesting to continue that
contrast by comparing the former service of Martha with
the present service of Mary.   The form in which Martha
then expressed her respect or affection was in dishes prepared for the table; Mary now pours a precious flask of
perfume upon the head and feet of her Lord.   The amount
which Martha attempted to do was declared by Jesus to
be unnecessary; the prodigal expenditure of Mary receives
his approval.   The spirit of Martha was that of trouble
and anxiety and jealous complaint; the motive of Mary is
gratitude and passionate, self-forgetful love.

It is not, however, with Martha that Mary is contrasted
in this last picture, but rather with Judas.   Her motive,
just described, has as its foil the deceit and avarice of the
thief and traitor.

It is but six days before the death of Jesus.   A feast is
being given at Bethany in his honor, and in gratitude for
his raising Lazarus from the dead.   The latter is one of
the guests.   Martha is serving, and surely in a spirit of
peaceful gratitude and reverence.   Mary takes a pound
of ointment, and not only follows the custom of anointing
with oil the head of an honored guest, but lavishly pours
the perfume on the feet of Jesus, and then, in deepest
humility, wipes his feet with her hair.   Now it is that
Judas utters his cruel protest: "Why was not this ointment sold for three hundred shillings, and given to the
poor?"   "Now this he said, not because he cared for the
poor; but because he was a thief, and having the bag [i.e.,
serving as treasurer for the little band of disciples] took
away [i.e., stole] what was put therein."   How his hypocrisy and greed stand out against the pure, passionate
devotion of Mary!   Is it unkind to suspect sometimes the
motives of men who refuse to support evangelistic and
missionary work on the plea that it would be better to
spend money for charity?   Of course we must ever fulfill

our obligations to the poor; but in his rebuke of Judas, Jesus forever vindicates the most extravagant gifts which are made in devotion to him, and condemns the spurious philanthropy which is not animated by love for him: "Suffer her to keep it against the day of my burying. For the poor ye have always with you; but me ye have not always." True gifts to the poor are in the name of Christ, and for the sake of Christ, and to win men to Christ. Social service divorced from Christianity may spend the treasure of Mary according to the direction of Judas.

In her act of devotion, Jesus seemed to see that Mary had unconsciously rendered a greater service than she had supposed. The gift was no purposeless waste. It was in reality an embalming of his body for burial. His words suggest divine foresight, and spoken to Judas, they intimate that the cruel avarice of the traitor is about to cause the death of Jesus; while the deed of Mary shows how he is embalmed in the hearts of his followers, and is a prophecy of the devotion to him which will fill the world with the perfume of self-sacrificing love.

Mary was rebuked by Judas; but her brother Lazarus became the object of more deadly hatred. He was a living witness to the power of Christ, and because of his testimony many became believers. The story of the feast is therefore followed by the statement that "the chief priests took counsel that they might put Lazarus also to death." Is it strange that witnesses for Christ are hated by his enemies today?

(2) The Public Entry Into Jerusalem   Ch. 12:12-19

12 On the morrow a great multitude that had come to the feast, when they heard that Jesus was coming to Jerusalem, 13 took the branches of the palm trees, and went forth to meet him, and cried out, Hosanna: Blessed is he that cometh in the name of the Lord, even the King of Israel. 14 And Jesus, having found a young ass, sat thereon; as it is written, 15 Fear not, daughter of Zion: behold, thy

King cometh, sitting on an ass's colt. 16 These things un-derstood not his disciples at the first: but when Jesus was glorified, then remembered they that these things were writ-ten of him, and that they had done these things unto him. 17 The multitude therefore that was with him when he called Lazarus out of the tomb, and raised him from the dead, bare witness. 18 For this cause also the multitude went and met him, for that they heard that he had done this sign. 19 The Pharisees therefore said among them-selves, Behold how ye prevail nothing; lo, the world is gone after him.

John has produced many witnesses to the fact that Jesus is the Messiah, but none more picturesque than the multi-tudes who pay their homage to Jesus as he enters the Holy City on the day following the anointing at Bethany. Many features of the scene, reported by the other Gospels, are omitted; but no other account gives more explicitly the testimony of the festal throng to their belief that, in the person of Jesus, the predicted Messiah has appeared. They attest their faith in symbol and in song; they wave palm branches, the emblems of beauty and triumph and joy; they cry: "Hosanna: Blessed is he that cometh in the name of the Lord," thus using a psalm which all the Jews regarded as a prophecy of the coming Messiah (Ps. 118:26).

Jesus meets their confession of faith by as definite a claim. He fulfills in minute detail the prophecy relative to the coming Messiah, as he enters the city riding upon an ass. (Zech. 9:9.) This was his final and most open offer of himself to the nation as their King. The "hour" had come which his mother and brethren had impatiently desired, the "hour" of his royal manifestation to Israel; but it was to be followed by the "hour" of which he knew so well, the "hour" of his rejection and death, and the "hour" of his resurrection and exaltation.

The faith of the multitudes was imperfect. Little did they comprehend the true nature of his Person and his mission. Even the most intimate of his disciples did not understand the real meaning of the scene in which they were playing a conspicuous part: "These things understood not his disciples at the first: but when Jesus was glorified, then remembered they that these things were written of him, and that they had done these things unto him." Strange mingling of sorrow and of joy, that memory must have been! They saw how imperfectly they had seen, they knew how little they had known, they "understood" how they had not understood; but they remembered, too, how exactly they had fulfilled the divine prophecy, how close they had been to the person of the King. Thus memory brings its remorse, when we recall how blind we were to beauties so bright, to the true meaning of experiences most precious, to the value of friends now gone; but so, too, it has its blessedness, when we look back over the journey and see that it was planned by a divine Master, or as we review the experiences of the long years and see in them the fulfillment of his eternal purposes of love.

John closes his narrative with a note found in no other Gospel, and quite in keeping with his continual purpose. He intimates that the faith of the multitudes was due, in largest measure, to the "sign" of the raising of Lazarus: and that the unparalleled popularity of Jesus only goads his enemies, the rulers, to follow as soon as possible the desperate counsel of Caiaphas, and to compass the death of Christ. How continually is John contrasting the expressions of faith and unbelief!

(3) The Last Ministry in the Temple   Ch. 12:20-36

20 Now there were certain Greeks among those that went up to worship at the feast: 21 these therefore came to Philip, who was of Bethsaida of Galilee, and asked him, saying, Sir, we would see Jesus. 22 Philip cometh and telleth Andrew: Andrew cometh, and Philip, and they tell Jesus. 23 And Jesus answereth them, saying, The hour is come, that the Son of man should be glorified. 24 Verily,

verily, I say unto you, Except a grain of wheat fall into the earth and die, it abideth by itself alone; but if it die, it beareth much fruit. 25 He that loveth his life loseth it; and he that hateth his life in this world shall keep it unto life eternal. 26 If any man serve me, let him follow me; and where I am, there shall also my servant be: if any man serve me, him will the Father honor. 27 Now is my soul troubled; and what shall I say? Father, save me from this hour. But for this cause came I unto this hour. 28 Father, glorify thy name. There came therefore a voice out of heaven, saying, I have both glorified it, and will glorify it again. 29 The multitude therefore, that stood by, and heard it, said that it had thundered: others said, An angel hath spoken to him. 30 Jesus answered and said, This voice hath not come for my sake, but for your sakes. 31 Now is the judgment of this world: now shall the prince of this world be cast out. 32 And I, if I be lifted up from the earth, will draw all men unto myself. 33 But this he said, signifying by what manner of death he should die. 34 The multitude therefore answered him, We have heard out of the law that the Christ abideth for ever: and how sayest thou, The Son of man must be lifted up? who is this Son of man? 35 Jesus therefore said unto them, Yet a little while is the light among you. Walk while ye have the light, that darkness overtake you not: and he that walketh in the darkness knoweth not whither he goeth. 36 While ye have the light, believe on the light, that ye may become sons of light.

These things spake Jesus, and he departed and hid himself from them.

From among all the memorable incidents of Passion Week only one is selected by John; it is recorded by no other writer, but it is distinctly in accordance with the purpose of this Gospel. Certain Greeks request an interview with Jesus; and in his reply our Lord gives testimony to his divine nature by his knowledge of the future, he intimates the self-sacrifice involved in faith, and testifies to the glory of the life in which faith issues. These Greeks were probably proselytes to Judaism; they may have come from only the Greek cities of Galilee; but to the mind of Christ, and so of John, they were the representatives of the whole Gentile world. Their request, following the story of the devotion of Mary, and of the hosannas of the multitudes, is the supreme proof of the love and faith and interest aroused by the public ministry of Christ; it further gave occasion for a prophecy of the universal blessings to result from the mission of Christ, which, in the view of John, always concerns the whole world. This mission, however, will be accomplished only by death and resurrection. Therefore, in his reply to the request of the Greeks, our Lord emphasizes the supreme character of the "hour" which has struck.

We are not told whether or not the Greeks were brought into his presence; but his words are a real reply to their request: "You would see me," he seems to say; "then you have arrived at exactly the right time, for the hour has come for the Son of man to be glorified." In his death and resurrection he is to be revealed in his true character, as the Savior of the world. The Greeks did not need to hear his words or to see his miracles; his death was what they needed to witness. His cross would be the attractive power which would draw to himself all those multitudes of the Gentile world represented by these inquirers.

Jesus illustrates the absolute necessity of his death by a reference to nature (v. 24); a grain of wheat must first be buried, its coverings must decay, it must perish as a grain before it can produce a multitude of grains like itself. He applies to himself (v. 25) this great law of life through death, of service and influence through self-sacrifice, and declares that should he seek selfishly to avoid the cross, he would forfeit all that was worthy the name "life"; but by yielding up his life, he would secure and bestow blessings that are eternal. This same law he applies to his disciples. (V. 26.) In contrast to the Greek ideal of self-gratification, his servants must follow him in the path of self-denial, not merely with a view to self-realization, and not first of all for the sake of others, but for the sake of Christ. The result will be a broadening life, an enlarging influence, and also an abiding fellowship with Christ, and the divine approval of his Father. "And I, if I be lifted up . . . , will draw all men unto myself." This does not mean universal salvation, nor refer primarily to the ultimate triumph of Christ. "All men" refers to the Greeks, and to those of all the nations whom they represented. Not only Jews were to be drawn to Christ, but also Gentiles; that is "all men" without distinction, not without exception.

The attractive power was to be his cross. The lifting up of Christ has no reference to preaching. He was to be "lifted up," not by testimony nor by imitating his life; but in his death: "This he said, signifying by what manner of death he should die." The cross is still the supreme moral magnet of the world. It is not the teachings of Christ, nor his example, unrelated to his death, but his cross that is attracting multitudes and making them willing, as devoted followers, to take up the cross and come after him.

The people were puzzled by his plain prediction of death. They expected the Messiah to assume political rule and to abide in endless power; they did not understand the prior necessity of his death. The offense of the cross has not ceased. Men are still troubled by the truth relative to a crucified Savior. It is natural, however, to shrink from the suffering involved in the complete surrender of self. Pain is not pleasing; death is not a delight. In spite of all that is to be secured, Jesus trembles at the sight of the cross. He sees its necessity; but he is not blind to its anguish. "Now is my soul troubled; and what shall I say? Father, save me from this hour." There is all the agony of Gethsemane in this bitter cry; and, in the words which follow, all its victory, too: "But for this cause came I unto this hour. Father, glorify thy name."

"There came . . . a voice out of heaven, saying, I have . . . glorified it," that is, in the ministry of Jesus, "and will glorify it again," that is, in his death and resurrection and in their results. (V. 28.)   This voice the people could not understand; but Jesus declared that it had been uttered for their sakes.   It was designed to make them realize the supreme importance of his death.   (Vs. 29-30.) This death was to be "the judgment of this world"; by it, the moral character of the world would be revealed and its sin condemned.   The prince of this world would "be cast out," for by it Satan was to receive his defeat, and through it his final overthrow.   (V. 31.)

Jesus does not now tarry for explanation.   He gives to the world one final warning and promise: "While ye have the light, believe on the light, that ye may become sons of light."   He is himself "the light of the world."   Whatever the problems or the mysteries involved in his Person and work, we must believe him, follow him, commit ourselves to him; otherwise we shall be like men stumbling along in a pathless night; but faith in him will transform us more and more into his likeness.   "These things spake Jesus, and he departed and hid himself from them."   His public ministry was at an end.

b. The Condemnation of Unbelief   Ch. 12:37-50

37 But though he had done so many signs before them, yet they believed not on him: 38 that the word of Isaiah the prophet might be fulfilled, which he spake,

Lord, who hath believed our report?

And to whom hath the arm of the Lord been revealed? 39 For this cause they could not believe, for that Isaiah said again, 40 He hath blinded their eyes, and he hardened their heart;

Lest they should see with their eyes, and perceive with their heart,

And should turn,

And I should heal them.

41 These things said Isaiah, because he saw his glory; and he spake of him.   42 Nevertheless even of the rulers many believed on him; but because of the Pharisees they did not

confess it, *lest they should be put out of the synagogue:
43 for they loved the glory* that is *of men more than the
glory* that is *of God.*

*44 And Jesus cried and said, He that believeth on me,
believeth not on me, but on him that sent me. 45 And he
that beholdeth me beholdeth him that sent me. 46 I am
come a light into the world, that whosoever believeth on
me may not abide in the darkness. 47 And if any man
hear my sayings, and keep them not, I judge him not: for
I came not to judge the world, but to save the world.
48 He that rejecteth me, and receiveth not my sayings,
hath one that judgeth him: the word that I spake, the same
shall judge him in the last day. 49 For I spake not from
myself; but the Father that sent me, he hath given me a
commandment, what I should say, and what I should speak.
50 And I know that his commandment is life eternal: the
things therefore which I speak, even as the Father hath
said unto me, so I speak.*

As the writer now pauses to glance backward over the
ministry of Jesus, he aims to emphasize the causes and
the consequences of Jewish unbelief. This he does in two
brief paragraphs, in one of which he employs largely the
words of the prophet Isaiah; and in the other the words of
Jesus. However, as in every section of the Gospel, he
presents testimony to the Person of our Lord. In quoting
from Isaiah he actually identifies Jesus as the same divine
Being whom Isaiah saw in his vision, even as the "Jehovah" of the Old Testament. (V. 41.) This same identity
with God, Jesus claims for himself, in words quoted from
his lips. Then, too, he suggests the issues of faith in a life
of spiritual vision, and of endless blessedness. (Vs. 46,
50.) The main burden of the two paragraphs, however,
is a condemnation of unbelief.

In the first paragraph (vs. 37-43) John refers to the
miracles of Jesus as sufficient to produce faith in him. In
the light of such signs, unbelief was sinful; but how could
it be explained? On the same grounds as unbelief can
always be explained, namely, spiritual blindness and moral

cowardice. The former was in the nature of a judicial blindness; the Jews would not believe, so a time came, as it always does, when they could not believe. Such was true in the days of Isaiah, and such in the days of Jesus.

Then, too, their hearts were not right: "They loved the glory that is of men more than the glory that is of God." Even when a partial faith had been awakened, it could neither be confessed nor developed because of the fear of human opposition or of the loss of social prestige. No one can ever hope to see the truth who is not willing to accept the consequences which its acceptance may bring; and continued unwillingness to believe results in the atrophy of the very faculty of faith.

The baleful consequences of unbelief are stated in the second paragraph. (Vs. 44-50.) This was not a discourse delivered by our Lord on some unknown occasion; but, as in the previous paragraph the writer has dwelt upon the works of Jesus, here he dwells upon his words, and gives a summary of his teachings to emphasize the solemn consequences of unbelief. Jesus has claimed to be a personal manifestation of God, and to have proclaimed the very will of God. Therefore, to reject Jesus is to reject God. During his earthly ministry Jesus refrained from pronouncing judgment upon men; but by their refusal to believe on him men were continually judging themselves, and "in the last day" they would be convicted by the very words which he had spoken. How can one who willfully rejects Jesus hope for acceptance with God? With such judgments upon unbelief, pronounced by John and by Jesus, the first half of our study of the Gospel closes, and the reader is privileged to turn to the bright contrast of the triumph of faith, with which the remainder of the book is chiefly concerned.

III
THE REVELATION TO THE DISCIPLES, AND THE CULMINATION OF FAITH AND UNBELIEF

Chs. 13 to 20

A. THE PRIVATE TEACHING Chs. 13 to 17

As we begin the thirteenth chapter of John we enter "the holy place" in the sacred structure of this Gospel, and during the narrative of five successive chapters we find ourselves alone with our Lord and his disciples. It is the night on which Jesus is betrayed. His public ministry has ended. The morrow will witness his anguish and death. He withdraws with "the twelve," to an "upper room," to eat with them the Passover feast, to institute his own memorial "supper," to reveal to his followers his matchless love, and to prepare them for the separation which he knows to be near. The main portion of the narrative is occupied with words of comfort and farewell. These, however, are preceded by two significant acts, and are followed by an intercessory prayer. These acts are necessary preliminaries to the discourses which are to be delivered; they consist in the moral preparation of heart produced by washing the disciples' feet, and in the dismissal from their company of the traitor, Judas.

1. THE MINISTRY OF LOVE   Ch. 13

a. Washing the Disciples' Feet   Ch. 13:1-20

1 Now before the feast of the passover, Jesus knowing that his hour was come that he should depart out of this

*world unto the Father, having loved his own that were in
the world, he loved them unto the end.   2 And during supper, the devil having already put into the heart of Judas
Iscariot, Simon's son, to betray him, 3 Jesus, knowing that
the Father had given all things into his hands, and that he
came forth from God, and goeth unto God, 4 riseth from
supper, and layeth aside his garments; and he took a towel,
and girded himself.   5 Then he poureth water into the
basin, and began to wash the disciples' feet, and to wipe
them with the towel wherewith he was girded.   6 So he
cometh to Simon Peter.   He saith unto him, Lord, dost
thou wash my feet?   7 Jesus answered and said unto him,
What I do thou knowest not now; but thou shalt understand hereafter.   8 Peter saith unto him, Thou shalt never
wash my feet.   Jesus answered him, If I wash thee not,
thou hast no part with me.   9 Simon Peter saith unto
him, Lord, not my feet only, but also my hands and my
head.   10 Jesus saith to him, He that is bathed needeth
not save to wash his feet, but is clean every whit: and ye
are clean, but not all.   11 For he knew him that should betray him; therefore said he, Ye are not all clean.*

*12 So when he had washed their feet, and taken his gar-
ments, and sat down again, he said unto them, Know ye
what I have done to you?   13 Ye call me, Teacher, and,
Lord: and ye say well; for so I am.   14 If I then, the Lord
and the Teacher, have washed your feet, ye also ought to
wash one another's feet.   15 For I have given you an example, that ye also should do as I have done to you.
16 Verily, verily, I say unto you, A servant is not greater
than his lord; neither one that is sent greater than he that
sent him.   17 If ye know these things, blessed are ye if ye
do them.   18 I speak not of you all: I know whom I have
chosen: but that the scripture may be fulfilled, He that
eateth my bread lifted up his heel against me.   19 From
henceforth I tell you before it come to pass, that, when it
is come to pass, ye may believe that I am he.   20 Verily,
verily, I say unto you, He that receiveth whomsoever I
send receiveth me; and he that receiveth me receiveth him
that sent me.*

On the way to the room which had been prepared for
the paschal supper, or as the disciples were seating them-

selves at the table, a dispute had arisen as to who among them was the greatest. Jesus takes the occasion to remind them that, among his followers, greatness is measured by service, and then he gives them a memorable object lesson; he "riseth from supper, and layeth aside his garments; and he took a towel, and girded himself. Then he poureth water into the basin, and began to wash the disciples' feet, and to wipe them with the towel wherewith he was girded."

John prefaces the story of this memorable act by several phrases which emphasize its incomparable humility and intimate something of its meaning. He declares that it was just "before the feast of the passover." That note of time indicates that we have begun a new portion of the narrative, we have reached the period toward which we have been pointed continually, we are now to read of events which are connected with the death of Christ, and which are the fulfillment of all that the Passover feast and the offering of the paschal lamb symbolized. The very act of washing his disciples' feet was to be a picture of that voluntary humiliation whereby he had laid aside his "existence-form as God," had assumed the garment of human flesh, had taken the place of a servant, had even stooped to the death of the cross, that he might cleanse his followers from sin. John further states that Jesus was conscious "that his hour was come that he should depart out of this world unto the Father"; but even then he was self-forgetful and mindful only of the needs of his disciples. The motive of our Lord which the act so strikingly illustrates is declared to be perfect, unfailing love: "Having loved his own that were in the world, he loved them unto the end." This motive is even further emphasized by the statement which suggests that Jesus did not shrink from washing the feet even of the traitor, "the devil having already put into the heart of Judas Iscariot, Simon's son, to betray him." Last of all, the supreme humility of the act is indicated by the assurance that Jesus was mindful of his universal power, of his divine origin and destiny: "Knowing that the Father

had given all things into his hands, and that he came forth
from God, and goeth unto God." Even with such a sublime consciousness, Jesus stooped to wash his disciples'
feet.

His act was interrupted by a notable dialogue between
himself and Peter, which reveals the spiritual significance
of the scene. The disciple is hesitating to allow his Master
to perform for him so menial a service; and even though
assured that Jesus has a purpose which Peter will understand afterward, he objects: "Thou shalt never wash my
feet." Jesus replies: "If I wash thee not, thou hast no
part with me," indicating not only a part in the Passover
supper, but in the friendship of Jesus, and in all that he was
that night to impart to his disciples. Peter now turns im-
pulsively to the other extreme: "Lord, not my feet only,
but also my hands and my head." And Jesus answered:
"He that is bathed needeth not save to wash his feet, but
is clean every whit." It is at once evident that Jesus refers
to a spiritual cleansing which he was seeking to effect. He
did wash his disciples' feet to give them physical comfort.
No servant had appeared, as the supper was served, to perform that usual, necessary task; no one of the disciples,
disputing as they were as to relative greatness, dared so to
humble himself as to perform this lowly service. Jesus
therefore washed his disciples' feet; but he did more: he
cleansed their hearts. As the disciples beheld his matchless humility, and as he touched their feet, all their envy
and bitterness and unkindness and wrath were gone. They
were ready then to listen to the marvelous discourses which
fell from his lips. He knew that the disciples loved him,
and that new life had been given them by his Spirit, but he
also recognized their need of having their present state of
mind altered. He was aware that the heart of one was
filled with deadly enmity: "Ye are clean, but not all. For
he knew him that should betray him." How comforting,
yet, how serious, is the message for us! Jesus knows that
we love him and trust him, and he does not reject us be-

cause of a sudden failure, or a single fault. We have been cleansed from the guilt and stain of sin; but we do need daily cleansing from daily defilement. This he is ready and able to give; and of this we are assured as we see him stooping to wash his disciples' feet. The act was followed by a word of explanation, in which Jesus makes plain to his disciples that they should imitate him in loving, lowly service, and aim to secure not merely the physical comfort of others, but their moral and spiritual cleansing as well: "For I have given you an example, that ye also should do as I have done to you." He declares the blessedness of such service: but recalls a prophecy which shows that from such blessedness one of their number, the traitor, will be excluded; the rest, however, will have the dignity of being thus the very representatives, not only of their Master, but of his Father.

b. The Dismissal of the Traitor   Ch. 13:21-30

21 When Jesus had thus said, he was troubled in the spirit, and testified, and said, Verily, verily, I say unto you, that one of you shall betray me.   22 The disciples looked one on another, doubting of whom he spake.   23 There was at the table reclining in Jesus' bosom one of his disciples, whom Jesus loved.   24 Simon Peter therefore beckoneth to him, and saith unto him, Tell us who it is of whom he speaketh.   25 He leaning back, as he was, on Jesus' breast saith unto him, Lord, who is it?   26 Jesus therefore answereth, He it is, for whom I shall dip the sop, and give it him.   So when he had dipped the sop, he taketh and giveth it to Judas, the son of Simon Iscariot.   27 And after the sop, then entered Satan into him.   Jesus therefore saith unto him, What thou doest, do quickly.   28 Now no man at the table knew for what intent he spake this unto him.   29 For some thought, because Judas had the bag, that Jesus said unto him, Buy what things we have need of for the feast; or, that he should give something to the poor.   30 He then having received the sop went out straightway: and it was night.

By washing the disciples' feet, Jesus removed from their hearts the mood and temper which would have made them unable to receive his word; one more act must be performed; he must remove from the circle the one unfaithful follower, the one unsympathetic hearer, before he could feel free to pour out before the disciples the full measure of his final message of mystery, of love, and of cheer.

He states plainly the fact to which he has again and again referred: "Verily, verily, I say unto you, that one of you shall betray me." The startled disciples are eager to learn who the traitor can be. By a simple sign Jesus makes it evident to Peter and John that the traitor is Judas. At the same time Jesus addresses Judas and commands him to delay no longer in carrying out his foul purpose; but in doing so he uses words which leave the mission of Judas unknown to the disciples: "What thou doest, do quickly." John tells us that Judas "went out straightway"; he adds significantly, "And it was night."

The character of Judas gives us the most pitiful picture of unbelief contained in the Gospel. His opportunities of knowing Christ were unsurpassed; but he resisted the Light, he cherished his sin of avarice, he was untouched by the matchless love of the Master who even stooped to wash his feet; and now, at the table, Jesus gave him a last sign of fellowship, there was a final struggle of soul, but Satan conquered, and Judas went out into the night of his eternal disgrace and doom.

As in the former act of washing his disciples' feet, Jesus revealed his divine love, so here he manifested his divine knowledge. As in both cases Jesus was preparing the way for his words of cheer, we may be reminded that the Master is never willing to speak to hearts filed with enmity for others, or lacking in loving sympathy for him.

c. Jesus Announces His Departure   Ch. 13:31-38

31 When therefore he was gone out, Jesus saith, Now is the Son of man glorified, and God is glorified in him; 32 and God shall glorify him in himself, and straightway shall he glorify him. 33 Little children, yet a little while I am with you. Ye shall seek me: and as I said unto the Jews, Whither I go, ye cannot come; so now I say unto you. 34 A new commandment I give unto you, that ye love one another; even as I have loved you, that ye also love one another. 35 By this shall all men know that ye are my disciples, if ye have love one to another.

36 Simon Peter saith unto him, Lord, whither goest thou? Jesus answered, Whither I go, thou canst not follow me now; but thou shalt follow afterwards. 37 Peter saith unto him, Lord, why cannot I follow thee even now? I will lay down my life for thee. 38 Jesus answereth, Wilt thou lay down thy life for me? Verily, verily, I say unto thee, The cock shall not crow, till thou hast denied me thrice.

Jesus naturally begins his farewell discourse by a statement of his departure (vs. 31-33), but he adds a command (vs. 34-35) and a warning (vs. 36-38). This announcement of his going away is stated, however, in terms which the disciples are slow to understand. He is to be "glorified," by which he means that he is to be revealed as the Savior, as the divine Son of God, by his death and resurrection and ascension, and by the gift of the Holy Spirit. He gives them as a parting word a "new commandment"; this was the old commandment in which Moses had summarized the whole law, but Jesus made it "new" by giving to it a new standard, and a new motive: "Love one another; even as I have loved you." His love was to be shown in his death for others; such self-sacrificing love shown by his followers would be the witness to the world of true discipleship.

Peter did not understand what Jesus meant by saying, "Whither I go, ye cannot come." He did understand the command to love. He thought that Jesus was about to undertake some dangerous journey upon earth. He therefore declares that his love is so great that he will follow, and that he is willing to lay down his life for his Master. Jesus gives the solemn warning that before the dawn, Peter will deny him thrice. He does predict, however, that Peter will follow him afterward. How weak his lonely disciples were to be; how much did they need the promises of the chapters which immediately follow! When the Spirit had been given in Pentecostal power, how truly did Peter follow his Master, even to the cross! It is by the power of the same Spirit that we can show the love of true disciples and without denying him can follow the footsteps of our Lord.

2. THE WORDS OF CHEER   Chs. 14 to 16

a. Jesus Comforts His Disciples   Ch. 14

Having announced to the disciples his approaching separation from them, Jesus now speaks to them words of cheer and counsel. These are contained in the conversations and addresses of chapters fourteen, fifteen, and sixteen. Each of these chapters is concerned with the three dominant truths of this Gospel, namely: witness to the divine nature of Christ, the character and development of faith in him, and the experiences and qualities of the life in which faith issues. It may be noted also that each of these chapters emphasizes one of these truths, and in the order named. As to the Person of our Lord, the record of no miracle could bear such testimony to his deity as the words which are recorded in the present chapter. Jesus claims to be one with God, to be worthy of trust as God, to be the sole Revealer of God, to be an abiding, personal presence, inseparable from the divine Spirit of God. These claims are part of the very fabric of the narrative, but are incidental to its immediate aim, which is to record the words of comfort which Jesus addressed to his disciples. These are contained in a dialogue in which the thought centers largely in the promise that Jesus is to be with his disciples in a real but spiritual presence.

The Coming Reunion   Vs. 1-3

1 Let not your heart be troubled: believe in God, believe also in me. 2 In my Father's house are many mansions; if it were not so, I would have told you; for I go to prepare a place for you. 3 And if I go and prepare a place for you, I come again, and will receive you unto myself; that where I am, there ye may be also.

This is the most natural word of cheer; separation is at hand, but there is to be a reunion, speedy and endless. "Let not your heart be troubled"; but surely there was reason for dismay. Jesus had just assured his followers that one of them would betray him, that Peter would deny him, and, most distressing of all, that he was about to go whither they could not come. In spite of all, they were to trust in the goodness of God, and in his own purposes of love; "believe in God, believe also in me." This is the one remedy for troubled hearts.

"In my Father's house are many mansions"; there is room for all, and a welcome for all, in that state and place whither Jesus is going. In case there was to be no reunion, no gathering in that heavenly home, he would not have so often suggested to his followers a blessed eternity of fellowship: "If it were not so, I would have told you."

"I go to prepare a place for you." By his death and ascension and glorification, he was opening a way of access to the Father, and to the bliss of his abode. "And if I go and prepare a place for you, I come again, and will receive you unto myself; that where I am, there ye may be also." The spiritual coming, which forms the substance of this and the two following chapters, was to result in the most intimate personal fellowship with Jesus, but it would find its consummation at his visible return in glory, and in the endless reunion in the Father's house.

The Way to the Father   Vs. 4-11

4 And whither I go, ye know the way.   5 Thomas saith unto him, Lord, we know not whither thou goest; how know we the way? 6 Jesus saith unto him, I am the way and the truth, and the life: no one cometh unto the Father, but by me. 7 If ye had known me, ye would have known my Father also: from henceforth ye know him, and have seen him. 8 Philip saith unto him, Lord, show us the Father, and it sufficeth us. 9 Jesus saith unto him, Have I been so long time with you, and dost thou not know me, Philip? he that hath seen me hath seen the Father; how sayest thou, Show us the Father? 10 Believest thou not that I am in the Father, and the Father in me? the words that I say unto you I speak not from myself: but the Father abiding in me doeth his works. 11 Believe me that I am in the Father, and the Father in me: or else believe me for the very works' sake.

"And whither I go, ye know the way." He had told them that he was going to the Father, and by the way of death and resurrection; but they were bewildered. They could not understand why he should die; they did not believe that he would die. Their confusion is voiced by Thomas: "Lord, we know not whither thou goest; how know we the way?" The question affords Jesus an opportunity of giving a spiritual and profound interpretation of his words. "The way to the Father," he seems to be saying, "for me, is by way of death, but for you, and for all men, I am the way, because I am the truth and the life. No one cometh unto the Father, but by me. If ye had known me, ye would have known my Father also: and from henceforth ye know him, and have seen him." Philip asks for a direct vision of the Father; and by his reply Jesus shows his distress that his disciples have not seen in him, already, a true Revelation of God. He declares that his oneness with the Father has been attested both by his words and his works.

The Continued Work   Vs. 12-14

12 Verily, verily, I say unto you, He that believeth on me, the works that I do shall he do also; and greater works than these shall he do; because I go unto the Father. 13 And whatsoever ye shall ask in my name, that will I do, that the Father may be glorified in the Son. 14 If ye shall ask anything in my name, that will I do.

Another ground for comfort is stated in the promise that his going away is not to end the work which Jesus has begun. Believers are to perform greater works than even his miracles—not more marvelous in the judgment of the world, but of a higher character and a vaster extent. This is to be made possible because he is to go to the Father, and, as he proceeds to explain, is to send the Holy Spirit to work in and through his followers. This work is to be accomplished in answer to prayer which is to be offered in his name. By this last phrase Jesus means in virtue of, and in acceptance of, all that he has been revealed to be, as the divine Son of God, one with the Father. The promises to answer prayer are unlimited, except by the clear statements made on other occasions that prayer must be in faith, which includes submission, and in accordance with the will of God, both of which conditions are implied by the phrase, "In my name."

The Coming of the Comforter   Vs. 15-27

15 If ye love me, ye will keep my commandments. 16 And I will pray the Father, and he shall give you another Comforter, that he may be with you for ever, 17 even the Spirit of truth: whom the world cannot receive; for it beholdeth him not, neither knoweth him: ye know him; for he abideth with you, and shall be in you. 18 I will not leave you desolate: I come unto you. 19 Yet a little while,

*and the world beholdeth me no more; but ye behold me:
because I live, ye shall live also. 20 In that day ye shall
know that I am in my Father, and ye in me, and I in you.
21 He that hath my commandments, and keepeth them, he
it is that loveth me: and he that loveth me shall be loved
of my Father, and I will love him, and will manifest myself
unto him. 22 Judas (not Iscariot) saith unto him, Lord,
what is come to pass that thou wilt manifest thyself unto
us, and not unto the world? 23 Jesus answered and said
unto him, If a man love me, he will keep my word: and
my Father will love him, and we will come unto him, and
make our abode with him. 24 He that loveth me not keepeth not my words: and the word which ye hear is not mine,
but the Father's who sent me.*

25 These things have I spoken unto you, while yet *abiding with you. 26 But the Comforter,* even *the Holy Spirit,
whom the Father will send in my name, he shall teach you
all things, and bring to your remembrance all that I said
unto you. 27 Peace I leave with you; my peace I give
unto you: not as the world giveth, give I unto you. Let
not your heart be troubled, neither let it be fearful.*

The supreme ground of comfort, and the main message
of the chapter, is found in the promise: "I will pray the
Father, and he shall give you another Comforter, that he
may be with you for ever." The word "Comforter" or
"Paraclete," or "Advocate," as it is at times translated,
means "one who is called to the side of another" to give
help, protection, deliverance. This promised Comforter
was the Holy Spirit, and his various offices and functions,
as related to believers, are all summed up in the little word
"another." That is to say, Jesus had been a true "Comforter" for the disciples; now that his bodily presence was
to be withdrawn, his Spirit was to do for his disciples all
that Jesus had been doing for them. He was to guide, to
inspire, to strengthen, to sanctify. This promise of the
gift of the Holy Spirit does not imply that he was not on
earth already. He had ever been in the world, and had
always been performing the same work for the people of

God; but after the ascension of Christ, the Spirit was to manifest himself in new power; he was to have, as an instrument, the truth concerning a crucified, risen, Lord; and the resulting work of the Spirit was to be like a new "coming," a new "gift." His manifestation was to be conditioned upon loving obedience to Christ. (Vs. 15, 21.) His presence was to be continuous: "That he may be with you for ever." Here Jesus is not contrasting the action of the Spirit in former ages with that in the new age, but the abiding of the Spirit is contrasted with his own approaching departure by way of death and resurrection. The Comforter is further called "the Spirit of truth." The world, because of its lack of moral sympathy with Christ, will not be able to receive or recognize this Spirit. This Spirit was even then abiding in all fullness in the Master, and was so to dwell in his followers. (V. 17.)

In this coming of the Spirit, Christ himself returns to earth, and as a result of his coming the disciples will enjoy a larger life and a fuller knowledge of the Father and the Son. (Vs. 18-20.)

As Jesus is interrupted by the question as to how it is that he, the true Messiah, is to be manifested only to the disciples and not to the world, Jesus replies that the manifestation of which he has been speaking is spiritual; it is conditioned upon obedience to Christ, and its result will be a veritable abiding, in the believer, of the Father and the Son. (Vs. 22-23.) Jesus further assures his followers that the Comforter, whom he now clearly designates as "the Holy Spirit," will teach them all things and bring to their remembrance all the words of their Master. (Vs. 25-26.) In view of such promises, Jesus bequeaths to his disciples a legacy which he takes from the treasure house of his own experience: "Peace I leave with you; my peace I give unto you. . . . Let not your heart be troubled, neither let it be fearful."

The Necessary Separation   Vs. 28-31

*28 Ye heard how I said to you, I go away, and I come
unto you. If ye loved me, ye would have rejoiced, because
I go unto the Father: for the Father is greater than I.
29 And now I have told you before it come to pass, that,
when it is come to pass, ye may believe.   30 I will no more
speak much with you, for the prince of the world cometh:
and he hath nothing in me;   31 but that the world may
know that I love the Father, and as the Father gave me
commandment, even so I do.   Arise, let us go hence.*

Jesus adds a single word of comfort.   In spite of his
promised spiritual return, the disciples were to endure the
anguish of seeing him depart by way of death.   They were
to lose his bodily presence.   Jesus assures them therefore
that his going away was a necessary condition of his spiritual return; that his very prediction of death would later
strengthen their faith; that while they were now to separate, and Satan was to assault him, he was to gain no abiding victory, but only to aid in manifesting to the world the
loving obedience of the Son to the will of his Father.   In
these last sentences Jesus uses the phrase, "The Father is
greater than I," and it has been interpreted as intimating
that he did not claim actual deity; but could any mere
man, unless insane or blasphemous, use those words in
comparing himself with God?   It is true that the Son, in
the mystery of his relation to the Father, was, in the days
of his flesh, or in his eternal Sonship, subordinate to the
Father; but these words, like many in this sublime chapter, are true witnesses to the conscious deity of the God-
Man, Jesus Christ our Lord.

b. *Jesus the True Vine   Ch. 15:1-17*

*1 I am the true vine, and my Father is the husbandman.
2 Every branch in me that beareth not fruit, he taketh it
away: and every branch that beareth fruit, he cleanseth it,*

that it may bear more fruit. 3 Already ye are clean because of the word which I have spoken unto you. 4 Abide in me, and I in you. As the branch cannot bear fruit of itself, except it abide in the vine; so neither can ye, except ye abide in me. 5 I am the vine, ye are the branches: He that abideth in me, and I in him, the same beareth much fruit: for apart from me ye can do nothing. 6 If a man abide not in me, he is cast forth as a branch, and is withered; and they gather them, and cast them into the fire, and they are burned. 7 If ye abide in me, and my words abide in you, ask whatsoever ye will, and it shall be done unto you. 8 Herein is my Father glorified, that ye bear much fruit; and so shall ye be my disciples. 9 Even as the Father hath loved me, I also have loved you: abide ye in my love. 10 If ye keep my commandments, ye shall abide in my love; even as I have kept my Father's commandments, and abide in his love. 11 These things have I spoken unto you, that my joy may be in you, and that your joy may be made full. 12 This is my commandment, that ye love one another, even as I have loved you. 13 Greater love hath no man than this, that a man lay down his life for his friends. 14 Ye are my friends, if ye do the things which I command you. 15 No longer do I call you servants; for the servant knoweth not what his lord doeth: but I have called you friends; for all things that I heard from my Father I have made known unto you. 16 Ye did not choose me, but I chose you, and appointed you, that ye should go and bear fruit, and that your fruit should abide: that whatsoever ye shall ask of the Father in my name, he may give it you. 17 These things I command you, that ye may love one another.

To comfort his disciples, on the eve of his departure, our Lord had been assuring them that while he was indeed to go away, still, by his Spirit, he would be an abiding presence with them, and through them his work would be continued. This same truth he further illustrated by the figure of a vine and its branches. The disciples were to be in vital union with their unseen Lord, and through them his life was to be manifested and his purpose accomplished; just as the branches are in living connection with the vine, which, only on its branches, bears its fruit. As the previous chapter bore witness to Christ as a divine Being who would ever abide in his followers, so here, stress is laid upon the need of faith in him as the absolute condition of the life which he would impart. Faith is here pictured as an abiding in Christ, which is to be as inseparable as the union of a living branch and its vine; the result will be rich fruit of spiritual experience, of Christian virtues, of souls saved.

Jesus first expresses the displeasure of his Father toward his faithless followers: "Every branch in me that beareth not fruit, he taketh it away"; and he then mentions the provision for strengthening the spiritual life of true believers: "And every branch that beareth fruit, he cleanseth it, that it may bear more fruit." Both figures refer to the process of pruning; dead wood is cut away, and even living shoots and fruit-bearing branches are cut back, in order that the clusters of grapes may be more rich and full. So God, by his providences, does discipline Christians; and so it is necessary that our natural tendencies and actions and desires must be restrained, that the virtues of our Lord may be manifested in us and his work wrought through us. However, the instrument here suggested by which this pruning is accomplished, is not divine Providence but the teachings and the manifested will of Christ: "Already ye are clean because of the word which I have spoken unto you." The disciples, who had received this word, were cleansed, in principle, and potentially; but in experience every follower of Christ must apply to his own life this pruning knife, if fruit is to be produced in character and service.

The supreme condition of fruitfulness, however, is abiding in Christ; as the branches draw sap from the vine, so believers must derive their strength and wisdom and holiness and power from their present, divine, Lord: "Abide in me, and I in you. As the branch cannot bear fruit of itself, except it abide in the vine; so neither can ye, except ye abide in me." The faith in Christ thus symbolized is not, however, separated from "the word" to which reference was first made. The figure of speech has changed, but abiding in Christ has, as its very essence, obedience to him and submission to his word.

Before dwelling at length upon this condition of fruitfulness, Jesus again expresses the divine displeasure with lifeless branches, which are to be "cast forth" and "withered" and "burned." The thought is not to be so pressed as to raise the question of the loss of souls who are once united with Christ. We are concerned here with service rather than salvation. The words, however, are not without serious implications as to the absolute necessity of a real and continuous union with Christ.

This union, if characterized by a true submission to the will of Christ, is certain to result in fruitfulness: "If ye abide in me, and my words abide in you, ask whatsoever ye will, and it shall be done unto you." Here a new element is introduced, namely, prayer; but the relation is vital. One who is united with Christ in trustful obedience, one who meditates upon his word, one who is guided by his indwelling Spirit, will be led to pray for the success of the divine work in his own experience and in the world, and, for prayer so originating, there is no limit to its power. Fruitfulness must result; God will be glorified and believers will thus show themselves to be true disciples. (V. 8.)

As Jesus further urges his followers to abide in him, he slightly changes the figure and declares that they must abide in his love. He thus emphasizes anew the element of obedience, as characterizing true faith; only by obedience can we know and appreciate and abide in the love of Christ: "If ye keep my commandments, ye shall abide in my love." This surely will produce fruitfulness; this love is like sunlight to the ripening fruit. The result which Jesus specifies is "joy": "These things have I spoken unto you, . . . that your joy may be made full." (V. 11.)

How frequently are we tempted to believe that sin will produce happiness! Joy is the flower of right; it is always and only the fruit of obedience to Christ, and in its essence it is a consciousness of his approving love.

Last of all Jesus concentrates all his commandments in the one law of love: "This is my commandment, that ye love one another, even as I have loved you." (V. 12.) He illustrates this love by his own self-sacrifice which was to be consummated the next day upon the cross, and by his divine friendship which had led him to confide in his disciples all his plans and gracious purposes, and by the very work to which he had called them, a work which would consist in revealing true virtues and in the salvation of immortal souls, a work which would be accomplished by prayer in his holy name. It may be that some of us, who wonder at our fruitlessness, as followers of Christ, need this word of the Master: "These things I command you, that ye may love one another."

c. The Enmity of the World and the Work of the Spirit
Chs. 15:18 to 16:15

After the loving exhortation contained in the allegory of "the true vine," Jesus gives to his disciples a word of warning and also of encouragement. In spite of the beautiful fruit of Christian character, the disciples would be hated by the world; even while, in the name of Christ, they offered eternal life, the world would seek to put them to death; nevertheless, in their persecution and peril, they would be sustained by the Holy Spirit, who would triumph over the spirit of the world, and would give the disciples fuller revelation of truth. Such is in substance the content of this paragraph. Its thoughts center upon the great truths of this Gospel. It bears testimony to the Person of Christ by his expressed consciousness of equality with the Father and the divine Spirit; it intimates the development of faith and contains a solemn rebuke of unbelief; but it speaks most specifically of the life of believers as witnesses for their Lord.   The disciples had just been exhorted to abide in Christ, that they might bear fruit; here they are encouraged by the assurance that, in spite of the hostility of the world, abundant fruit would be produced through their testimony for the Master in the power of his indwelling Spirit.

(1) The Enmity of the World   Chs. 15:18 to 16:6

18 If the world hateth you, ye know that it hath hated me before it hated you.   19 If ye were of the world, the world would love its own: but because ye are not of the world, but I chose you out of the world, therefore the world hateth you.   20 Remember the word that I said unto you, A servant is not greater than his lord.   If they persecuted me, they will also persecute you; if they kept my word, they will keep yours also.   21 But all these things will they do unto you for my name's sake, because they know not him that sent me.   22 If I had not come and spoken unto them, they had not had sin: but now they have no excuse for their sin.   23 He that hateth me hateth my Father also.   24 If I had not done among them the works which none other did, they had not had sin: but now have they both seen and hated both me and my Father. 25 But this cometh to pass, that the word may be fulfilled that is written in their law, They hated me without a cause. 26 But when the Comforter is come, whom I will send unto you from the Father, even the Spirit of truth, which proceedeth from the Father, he shall bear witness of me: 27 and ye also bear witness, because ye have been with me from the beginning.

1 These things have I spoken unto you, that ye should not be caused to stumble.   2 They shall put you out of the synagogues: yea, the hour cometh, that whosoever killeth you shall think that he offereth service unto God.   3 And these things will they do, because they have not known the Father, nor me.   4 But these things have I spoken unto you, that when their hour is come, ye may remember them, how that I told you.   And these things I said not unto you

from the beginning, because I was with you. 5 But now
I go unto him that sent me; and none of you asketh me,
Whither goest thou?   6 But because I have spoken these
things unto you, sorrow hath filled your heart.

The enmity of the world is contrasted with the love of
believers, of which Jesus had just been speaking.   In a
Christian community, and wherever Christ is loved, his
followers will not be hated; but from those who reject
Christ and his claims, nothing need be expected but enmity, persecution, death; the servants will be hated just as
the Master was and just because of the Master.

This hatred is attributed to ignorance of God, to false
conceptions of his nature and will: "Yea, the hour cometh,
that whosoever killeth you shall think that he offereth
service unto God"; but it is further attributed to a willful,
stubborn, sinful ignorance of God, and to a hatred of
him as he has been revealed by Christ.   The clear testimony borne by the words and works of Christ had only
aggravated their guilt: "If I had not come and spoken unto
them, they had not had sin: but now they have no excuse
for their sin.   He that hateth me hateth my Father also.
If I had not done among them the works which none other
did, they had not had sin: but now have they both seen
and hated both me and my Father."   In no other part of
his Gospel has John declared more clearly the sinful nature
of unbelief, and the peril of rejecting Christ; for to deny
his claims and to refuse to become his disciple is to hate
God and to condemn one's own soul.

(2) The Work of the Spirit   Ch. 16:7-15

7 Nevertheless I tell you the truth: It is expedient for
you that I go away; for if I go not away, the Comforter
will not come unto you; but if I go, I will send him unto
you. 8 And he, when he is come, will convict the world
in respect of sin, and of righteousness, and of judgment:
9 of sin, because they believe not on me; 10 of righteous-

ness, because I go to the Father, and ye behold me no more; 11 of judgment, because the prince of this world hath been judged. 12 I have yet many things to say unto you, but ye cannot bear them now. 13 Howbeit when he, the Spirit of truth, is come, he shall guide you into all the truth: for he shall not speak from himself; but what things soever he shall hear, these shall he speak: and he shall declare unto you the things that are to come. 14 He shall glorify me: for he shall take of mine, and shall declare it unto you. 15 All things whatsoever the Father hath are mine: therefore said I, that he taketh of mine, and shall declare it unto you.

The work of the Holy Spirit has been mentioned more than once in the course of this Gospel, and notably in the previous chapters which spoke of the coming of the Comforter, but in no section of the narrative, possibly in no part of Scripture, is his work so clearly set forth as in this paragraph.

Jesus had told his disciples that he was going to the Father; he wished them to ask him more about this departure: "None of you asketh me, Whither goest thou?" Peter had asked but he had in mind something quite different, some perilous journey on earth; but the disciples were wholly concerned with their own sorrow at the coming separation. Jesus now assures them that the loss of his physical presence will be more than compensated by the coming of the Spirit. He did not mean that the Holy Spirit was not then present or had not always been in the world, but that, after the death and resurrection and ascension of Jesus, he would begin a work so marvelous and unique that it could properly be described under the figure of a "coming" or of a being "sent from the Father." This work would have as its very essence the making of Jesus known to his disciples in all the fullness of his divine Person and work: "He shall glorify me"; and through the disciples the making of Jesus known to the world: "He shall bear witness of me: and ye also bear witness." It is upon the work in the world accomplished through the disciples by the Spirit that Jesus first dwells (vs. 8-11), before enlarging upon the work of the Spirit within the disciples (vs. 12-15).

In the World   Vs. 7-11

It is true that the disciples are not here mentioned; the whole thought centers upon the mission of the Comforter; but they are the instruments by which he is to work; their witness is to be by his power; they are to be the voices by which he is to speak.   In fact, these verses are simply a statement of the result of the witness to Christ which his followers were to give, under the power of his Spirit.   He will reprove, or convince, or "convict," by the presentation of evidence: "He . . . will convict the world . . . of sin, and of righteousness, and of judgment."

(a) "Of sin, because they believe not on me."   This does not mean that unbelief is a sin; of course it is; but it means that the Holy Spirit will convict the world of being sinful, on the ground, or evidence, of its rejection of Christ. It is a sin not to believe in Christ; but the truth here taught is that the rejection of Christ shows one to be a sinner. Christ is good and holy and pure; to reject him is to convict onself of being opposed to goodness and holiness and purity and love.   When Christ is preached he becomes the Touchstone of character.

(b) "Of righteousness, because I go to the Father, and ye behold me no more"; that is, by his resurrection and ascension, Jesus was proved to be a righteous man, and all his claims to deity were vindicated.   The resurrection and ascension of Jesus still form the ground on which the Holy Spirit convinces men that Jesus is Christ, the Son of God.

(c) "Of judgment, because the prince of this world hath been judged."   The specific judgment in mind is that of the devil.   At the cross he massed all his forces, there he suffered his eternal defeat. His doom was settled and his sentence pronounced. Every time Christ is preached, under the power of the Holy Spirit, Satan suffers some further loss, and every saved soul is a new proof of his "judgment."

Thus we are concerned here with the sin of the world, the righteousness of Jesus, and the judgment of Satan, as these are proved by the Holy Spirit, on the evidence of the rejection of Jesus, of his resurrection, and of his triumph on the cross. These great facts, if presented by witnesses under the power of the Holy Spirit, never fail to convict the world. The first great fulfillment of the promise was on the Day of Pentecost when, as Peter, "filled with the Holy Spirit," presented these proofs, three thousand souls were convicted and saved. So today, when the Holy Spirit accomplishes a great work of saving grace, it is only where witnesses are testifying faithfully to a crucified, risen, ascended, divine Christ.

Within Believers   Vs. 12-15

This has been intimated already. It was summed up in the gracious words of Jesus: "I have yet many things to say unto you, but ye cannot bear them now," for until his death and resurrection there were many spiritual realities which his disciples would not be able to understand: "Howbeit when he, the Spirit of truth, is come, he shall guide you into all the truth: for he shall not speak from himself; but what things soever he shall hear, these shall he speak: and he shall declare unto you the things that are to come. He shall glorify me: for he shall take of mine, and shall declare it unto you. All things whatsoever the Father hath are mine." Thus, it is the office of the Comforter to reveal to the believer all the divine riches and grace that are in Christ Jesus, to take the great realities of his divine Person and work and make their meaning clear and vital. Nothing is said here of the consequent sanctifying influence in life and character; but we are concerned here with witnessing for Christ and are reminded that in preparation for such service we need the illumination and guidance of the Holy Spirit of truth.

d. The Encouraging Farewell Ch. 16:16-33

16 A little while, and ye behold me no more; and again a little while, and ye shall see me. 17 Some of his disciples therefore said one to another, What is this that he saith unto us, A little while, and ye behold me not; and again a little while, and ye shall see me: and, Because I go to the Father? 18 They said therefore, What is this that he saith, A little while? We know not what he saith. 19 Jesus perceived that they were desirous to ask him, and he said unto them, Do ye inquire among yourselves concerning this, that I said, A little while, and ye behold me not, and again a little while, and ye shall see me? 20 Verily, verily, I say unto you, that ye shall weep and lament, but the world shall rejoice: ye shall be sorrowful, but your sorrow shall be turned into joy. 21 A woman when she is in travail hath sorrow, because her hour is come: but when she is delivered of the child, she remembereth no more the anguish, for the joy that a man is born into the world. 22 And ye therefore now have sorrow: but I will see you again, and your heart shall rejoice, and your joy no one taketh away from you. 23 And in that day ye shall ask me no question. Verily, verily, I say unto you, If ye shall ask anything of the Father, he will give it you in my name. 24 Hitherto have ye asked nothing in my name: ask, and ye shall receive, that your joy may be made full.

25 These things have I spoken unto you in dark sayings: the hour cometh, when I shall no more speak unto you in dark sayings, but shall tell you plainly of the Father. 26 In that day ye shall ask in my name: and I say not unto you, that I will pray the Father for you; 27 for the Father himself loveth you, because ye have loved me, and have believed that I came forth from the Father. 28 I came out from the Father, and am come into the world: again, I leave the world, and go unto the Father. 29 His disciples say, Lo, now speakest thou plainly, and speakest no dark saying. 30 Now know we that thou knowest all things, and needest not that any man should ask thee: by this we believe that thou camest forth from God. 31 Jesus answered them, Do ye now believe? 32 Behold, the hour cometh, yea, is come, that ye shall be scattered, every man to his own, and shall leave me alone: and yet *I am not alone, because the Father is with me. 33 These things have I spoken unto you, that in me ye may have peace. In the world ye have tribulation: but be of good cheer; I have overcome the world.*

Now the last words are to be spoken. The time for separation has come. Jesus is going forth to betrayal and to death. Naturally he reverts to the subject of his departure; but his last message of comfort is the same in substance that he has already conveyed. He is going away, but he encourages his disciples by again assuring them that he is to be with them ever as an unseen, abiding presence. When the Holy Spirit has come in Pentecostal power, then the disciples will enjoy a truer, fuller fellowship with Christ than even in the days of his earthly ministry.

It is, in fact, with the work of the Holy Spirit that we are here concerned, as in the verses which precede. His agency, and the blessing he confers, is the very beginning and ending of the teaching of our Lord in the "upper room."

Thus when Jesus closes his farewell discourse he teaches (1) that the real manifestation of his spiritual presence, by the agency of the Holy Spirit, will speedily follow his death: "A little while, and ye behold me no more"; he was to die on the morrow. "Again a little while, and ye shall see me," not only in resurrection, but with enlarged spiritual vision, at Pentecost, and ever after.

As the disciples are puzzled at a promise so mysterious, which intimated that the going away of Jesus was a condition of his more real presence, he further reassures them by stating (2) that their temporary anguish at the separation caused by his death will be forgotten in the joy of the spiritual reunion which will be endless: "And ye therefore now have sorrow: but I will see you again, and your heart shall rejoice, and your joy no one taketh away from you."

(3) The influence of the Holy Spirit will further enlarge the knowledge of the disciples, as already suggested in verses 12-15. They will not need to make such inquiries of the Lord as they have made during this conversation: "And in that day ye shall ask me no question." (4) They will pray, however, but it will be to the Father in the name of the Son: "Hitherto have ye asked nothing in my name: ask, and ye shall receive, that your joy may be made full." "In my name" signifies in virtue of all he has been revealed to be; after Pentecost, as never before, he was known as the Christ, the Son of God, the risen, glorified, invisible, divine Lord and Savior. Prayer in his name would surely avail. (5) Jesus finally lays aside all figures of speech and plainly declares his divine preexistence, his incarnation, his death, his resurrection: "I came out from the Father, and am come into the world: again, I leave the world, and go unto the Father."

This, at last, the disciples seem to understand, and they assert their faith: "By this we believe that thou camest forth from God." Jesus replies (6) that their faith is to be sorely tested, and will not be victorious at first: "Behold, the hour cometh, yea, is come, that ye shall be scattered, every man to his own, and shall leave me alone." (7) However, united to him by a strengthened faith, by the power of his Spirit, they shall soon enjoy peace and share the victory of their Master over the opposition and enmity of the world.

This closing paragraph is in peculiar harmony with the continual purpose of John. As the fourteenth chapter presents testimony to the divine Person of Christ, as the fifteenth emphasizes the need of a vital faith by which believers can abide in him, so this chapter enlarges upon the life which results from faith, a life in which the Lord, by the power of his indwelling Spirit, makes real his gracious presence, gives increasing knowledge of the truth and confidence in prayer, inspires heroic courage, and secures abiding peace.

3. JESUS' INTERCESSORY PRAYER   Ch. 17:1-26

"There is no voice which has ever been heard, either in heaven or in earth, more exalted, more holy, more fruitful, more sublime, than this prayer offered up by the Son of God himself." Such are the words of Melanchthon; and such has been the verdict of the Christian centuries. This chapter constitutes "the most precious fragment of the past." Here, according to all commentators, we enter the Holy of Holies of the New Testament, for here we are given the most profound revelation of the very heart of our Lord.

This is, in very truth, "The Lord's Prayer." We properly apply this name to the formula taught by Jesus to his disciples, and beginning, "Our Father who art in heaven"; but speaking more strictly, this is his prayer; he could not have used the petitions he taught his disciples, including as they do a request for forgiveness; and none of his disciples could have uttered these words. If we wish one unanswerable argument to prove the deity of Christ, it can be supplied in this single chapter of John. The sublime self-consciousness of the speaker, his claim of universal dominion, his reference to a previous existence in living unity with the eternal God, leave us as the only possible explanations, either insanity, blasphemy, or deity. If on the other hand, we are not concerned with witness to the person of Christ but wish an answer to the question with which John is continually concerned, namely, what is the life in which faith in Christ will issue, we have here certain petitions offered, by the Son of God, for his followers; as they come from him, what are these but prophecies of blessing and promises to faith?

Jesus Prays to Be Glorified   Vs. 1-5

1 These things spake Jesus; and lifting up his eyes to heaven, he said, Father, the hour is come; glorify thy Son, that the Son may glorify thee: 2 even as thou gavest him authority over all flesh, that to all whom thou hast given him, he should give eternal life. 3 And this is life eternal, that they should know thee the only true God, and him whom thou didst send, even Jesus Christ. 4 I glorified thee on the earth, having accomplished the work which thou hast given me to do. 5 And now, Father, glorify thou me with thine own self with the glory which I had with thee before the world was.

Jesus prays, first of all for himself; but the petition is the farthest possible remove from selfishness. He prays to be glorified in order that he may glorify his Father, and thus give "eternal life" to his followers. "Father, the hour is come; glorify thy Son, that the Son may glorify thee: even as thou gavest him authority over all flesh, that to all whom thou hast given him, he should give eternal life."

"The hour" was the expected time of his death and resurrection. This prayer was uttered on the night of his agony only a few hours before his Passion. By his request to be glorified, Jesus referred to his crucifixion, his triumph over the grave, his ascension, and supremely his outpouring of the Holy Spirit. To "glorify" one is to make one known; Jesus desires to be made known in his true character, as the divine Son of God, as the Messiah, as the Savior of the world. This manifestation all centered in "the hour" which had come, but which would include Pentecost and all that the gift of the Holy Spirit suggests. That gift constituted or secured the answer to this prayer. By "the glory" of the Son, the glory of the Father was secured. God was never so fully revealed in all his justice and love and holiness and grace as by "the hour" with which we are now concerned.

Then, too, by this revelation, life was secured for the followers of Christ; for "this is life eternal, that they should know thee the only true God, and him whom thou didst send, even Jesus Christ." To "know," according to this Gospel, is not merely an act of the mind; in that sense, demons know God; but it denotes love, obedience, faith, the response of the entire being. Thus to know God as revealed in his Son is to have eternal life. This life is, therefore, not only a future, but a present experience; it denotes endless existence but also a heavenly blessedness. This first petition Jesus based upon the fact that his earthly task was complete: "I have accomplished the work which thou hast given me to do." Already the supreme sacrifice seemed to him to have been made. His work was finished; and he could therefore pray, "And now, Father, glorify thou me with thine own self with the glory which I had with thee before the world was."

How few of us feel, under the shadow of death, that life is complete, that its work is finished! What a pathetic series of beginnings and failures and imperfect endeavors it does seem to be. Yet, if one does the will of God, the symbol of life need not be a broken column. Much may seem incomplete: only three years of ministry, only a few sick healed, only a few sermons preached, only eleven disciples secured, no book written, no organization formed; but the work may be finished, we need not linger longer here; the cross remains, then glory.

Jesus Prays for His Disciples   Vs. 6-19

6 I manifested thy name unto the men whom thou gavest me out of the world: thine they were, and thou gavest them to me; and they have kept thy word. 7 Now they know that all things whatsoever thou hast given me are from thee: 8 for the words which thou gavest me I have given unto them; and they received them, and knew

*of a truth that I came forth from thee, and they believed
that thou didst send me.   9 I pray for them: I pray not for
the world, but for those whom thou hast given me; for they
are thine: 10 and all things that are mine are thine, and
thine are mine: and I am glorified in them.   11 And I am
no more in the world, and these are in the world, and I
come to thee.   Holy Father, keep them in thy name which
thou has given me, that they may be one, even as we* are.
*12 While I was with them, I kept them in thy name which
thou hast given me: and I guarded them, and not one of
them perished, but the son of perdition; that the scripture
might be fulfilled.   13 But now I come to thee; and these
things I speak in the world, that they may have my joy
made full in themselves.   14 I have given them thy word;
and the world hated them, because they are not of the
world, even as I am not of the world.   15 I pray not that
thou shouldest take them from the world, but that thou
shouldest keep them from the evil* one.   *16 They are not
of the world, even as I am not of the world.   17 Sanctify
them in the truth: thy word is truth.   18 As thou didst send
me into the world, even so sent I them into the world.   19
And for their sakes I sanctify myself, that they themselves
also may be sanctified in truth.*

Jesus prays next for his immediate disciples, for "the
twelve" who had been with him; but he first describes
them in phrases which have a meaning and a message for
all who call themselves his followers: "The men whom
thou gavest me out of the world," "they have kept thy
word"; "the words which thou gavest me . . . they received"; "they believed that thou didst send me."

For these men Jesus prays: "I pray not for the world,
but for those whom thou hast given me."   He does not
mean that he never prayed for the world, or that we should
not so pray; but on this supreme occasion he wishes to
ask certain things for his followers.

The petitions are two in number.   First he prays that
they may be kept from evil.   During the earthly ministry
of Jesus he has guarded his disciples, but now he is leav-

ing them. The world will hate them. He therefore commits them to the care of his Father. He does not ask that they shall be taken out of the world as he himself is leaving the world. He does not ask that they shall be kept from sorrow and pain and temptation, but from gloom and discouragement and sin. "I pray not that thou shouldest take them from the world, but that thou shouldest keep them from the evil one."

Their protection was to be effected by the agency of his Spirit, but also by the instrument of the truth concerning his Father. "While I was with them, I kept them in thy name," that is, by means of what God was known to be, by the revelation which Jesus had given of the Father; and by the same means they will be kept after his departure: "Holy Father, keep them in thy name which thou hast given me."

Secondly, Jesus prays that his disciples may be sanctified. This does not here refer specifically to holiness, or separation from sin. That was the burden of the first petition. The request is rather that they may be set apart for service, and more specifically for the service of witnessing to the truth. It is really a prayer for the consecration of his chosen messengers to their appointed mission. "Sanctify them in the truth: thy word is truth." The revelation of the Father which Jesus had given, "the truth" he had revealed, was to be not only the instrument of their consecration but the sphere of their service. Therefore Jesus adds, "As thou didst send me into the world, even so sent I them into the world," that is, to be his messengers, to testify to "the truth."

Jesus Prays for His Church   Vs. 20-26

20 Neither for these only do I pray, but for them also that believe on me through their word;   21 that they may all be one; even as thou, Father, art in me, and I in thee, that they also may be in us: that the world may believe that thou didst send me.   22 And the glory which thou hast

given me I have given unto them; that they may be one,
even as we are one; 23 I in them, and thou in me, that
they may be perfected into one; that the world may know
that thou didst send me, and lovedst them, even as thou
lovedst me. 24 Father, I desire that they also whom thou
hast given me be with me where I am, that they may be-
hold my glory, which thou hast given me: for thou lovedst
me before the foundation of the world. 25 O righteous
Father, the world knew thee not, but I knew thee; and
these knew that thou didst send me; 26 and I made known
unto them thy name, and will make it known; that the love
wherewith thou lovedst me may be in them, and I in them.

Having prayed for himself and his disciples, Jesus now
prays for all believers, "that they may all be one," and
that at last they may be with him in heavenly "glory."
The first petition, for the oneness of believers, refers to
something quite different, and far more wonderful, than
the "church unity," the "organic union," the "united
Christendom," to which it is commonly supposed to refer.
It contemplates a spiritual unity which must be given visible expression, but which in its essence, consists of a
union with Christ, and through him with God.   Jesus
prayed "that they also may be in us."   The prayer was
given its initial answer on the Day of Pentecost when, by
the Holy Spirit, believers were "all baptized into one
body."   So Paul does not pray for "church unity," but insists that it already exists.   Even now, "there is one body,"
composed of all who are united with Christ, as there is
"one Spirit, . . . one hope . . . ; one Lord, one faith,
one baptism, one God and Father of all."
There does remain, however, a further fulfillment of this
petition, and for it we are to work and to pray.   This
spiritual unity must be made manifest, and so manifest as
to be an irresistible argument for the divine mission of
Christ: "That the world may know that thou didst send
me."   What this ultimate expression may be, in this present age of imperfect knowledge, none is wise enough to

predict. There is little hope, perhaps no reasonable desire, for unity of organization, for uniformity of worship, for unanimity of creed; certainly not if any of these must be secured by compulsion, or by the sacrifice of conviction. There is, however, much that can be done by every believer: first, accept and act upon the reality of our vital union as members of the one body of Christ, whatever our particular "church" or "society" may be; secondly, remember that Christian unity can be advanced only by an increasing knowledge of Christ and of the truth which he reveals; thirdly, manifest the love, long-suffering, gentleness, meekness, and patience which are the fruit of the Spirit, and look to the guidance of that Spirit to lead us toward that manifestation of unity for which a lost world still waits.

A time is surely coming when this manifestation will be complete. "When Christ, who is our life, shall be manifested, then shall ye also with him be manifested in glory." It is with a petition for this future "glory" of the church that the prayer of Jesus reaches its climax. "Father, I desire that they also whom thou hast given me be with me where I am, that they may behold my glory, which thou hast given me." Of course believers enjoy a present glory: "The glory which thou hast given me I have given unto them," the glory of being children of God and possessors of eternal life; but there is greater blessedness in store for them, an actual vision of Christ, a share in the ineffable glory granted to the Son by the love of the Father. For such glory Jesus pleads on the ground of the faith of his followers, and of his continuing revelation to them, and of his own abiding presence with them. It is the last phrase, "I in them," which is the assurance and condition of the answer to this high-priestly prayer of intercession. The indwelling of Christ, by his Spirit, is the power and agent by whom his followers are being kept from sin, sanctified in service, given unity of life, made ready for glory.

B. THE SUPREME WITNESS   Chs. 18 to 20

1. THE BETRAYAL AND TRIAL   Chs. 18:1 to 19:16

As we review the closing scenes in the life of our Lord, we find the culminating witness to his divine Person in his victory over fear and pain and death; we also have the picture and promise of the larger life assured to his followers by his own resurrection; but it is the purpose of John so to rehearse the story as especially to exhibit the consummation of faith and unbelief.

The former is manifested in the confident joy of the disciples and especially in the belief of Thomas; the latter finds its expression in the mad hatred of the Jews which is consummated by the murder of Jesus.

This cruel unbelief is found, however, even in the little circle of the disciples; and there it appears even more hateful because of its contrast with the tender love of Jesus, and the peculiar opportunities for the development of faith.

a. The Betrayal and Arrest   Ch. 18:1-11

1 When Jesus had spoken these words, he went forth with his disciples over the brook Kidron, where was a garden, into which he entered, himself and his disciples.   2 Now Judas also, who betrayed him, knew the place: for Jesus ofttimes resorted thither with his disciples.   3 Judas then, having received the band of soldiers, *and officers from the chief priests and the Pharisees, cometh thither with lanterns and torches and weapons.   4 Jesus therefore, knowing all the things that were coming upon him, went forth, and saith unto them, Whom seek ye?   5 They answered him, Jesus of Nazareth.   Jesus saith unto them, I am* he.   *And Judas also, who betrayed him, was standing with them.   6 When therefore he said unto them, I am* he, *they went backward, and fell to the ground.   7 Again therefore he asked them, Whom seek ye?   And they said, Jesus of Nazareth.   8 Jesus answered, I told you that I am* he;

if therefore ye seek me, let these go their way: 9 that the
word might be fulfilled which he spake, Of those whom
thou hast given me I lost not one. 10 Simon Peter there-
fore having a sword drew it, and struck the high priest's
servant, and cut off his right ear. Now the servant's name
was Malchus. 11 Jesus therefore said unto Peter, Put up
the sword into the sheath: the cup which the Father hath
given me, shall I not drink it?

As Judas enters the Garden, whither our Lord had withdrawn to pray with his disciples, he is not to be regarded
as an inhuman monster, nor yet as an innocent and mis-
guided enthusiast. Both of these false extremes in the
interpretation of the character of Judas are held by modern
writers. The fact is that his development had been perfectly normal and natural; it is this which constitutes the
solemnity of the warning to the professed followers of
Christ. He is simply the illustration of a man who cher-
ishes a besetting sin, and yields to an evil passion, in the
face of warning and in spite of abundant light, until at last
he hates the light and takes his place on the side of the
enemies of Christ. Judas is an example of the triumph
of selfishness; and there is no one of the followers of Christ
who is incapable of traitorous thought, and who need not
be on his guard against treacherous deeds which may im-
peril the cause of his Master.

In striking contrast to the hideous spectacle of Judas
is the figure of Jesus, in his divine majesty and his loyal
love. He voluntarily offers himself to his enemies, knowing their murderous purpose, and his one thought is for
the safety of his followers. The soldiers are so awed by his
appearance that they fall to the ground. As they hesitate
to arrest him, he again offers himself to them but requests
that his disciples may be allowed their liberty. He feared
lest, should they share his fate, even in part, their faith
might fail. Our Lord never allows us to be too sorely
tempted, never beyond what we are able to endure. Peter
by a rash act attempts to defend his Lord by attacking
with a sword a servant of the high priest; he thus nearly

frustrates the purpose of the Master and compromises his cause.

Jesus rebukes him with a word full of deep significance, showing the voluntary character of his atoning death: "Put up the sword into the sheath: the cup which the Father hath given me, shall I not drink it?" What is this "cup"? Not, as some are asserting, mere physical death, but death as the bearer of sin. There are those who suggest that in his agony, a few moments before, Jesus feared that he might die in the Garden and so not reach the cross. Nothing could be farther from the truth. Jesus dreaded "the cup," not merely of physical death, but of death in the place of sinners. He did shrink from being "made to be sin" for us; from the mystery of that experience he asked to be delivered, but only for the brief hour; the victory was his, and here he steps forth to meet the traitor and his murderous band with a calm which is majestic and divine.

b. The Trial   Chs. 18:12 to 19:16

By the Jews   Ch. 18:12-27

12 So the band and the chief captain, and the officers of the Jews, seized Jesus and bound him, 13 and led him to Annas first; for he was father in law to Caiaphas, who was high priest that year. 14 Now Caiaphas was he that gave counsel to the Jews, that it was expedient that one man should die for the people.

15 And Simon Peter followed Jesus, and so did *another disciple. Now that disciple was known unto the high priest, and entered in with Jesus into the court of the high priest; 16 but Peter was standing at the door without. So the other disciple, who was known unto the high priest, went out and spake unto her that kept the door, and brought in Peter. 17 The maid therefore that kept the door saith unto Peter, Art thou also* one *of this man's disciples? He saith, I am not. 18 Now the servants and the officers were standing* there, *having made a fire of coals; for it was cold; and they were warming themselves: and*

Peter also was with them, standing and warming himself.

19 The high priest therefore asked Jesus of his disciples, and of his teaching. 20 Jesus answered him, I have spoken openly to the world; I ever taught in synagogues, and in the temple, where all the Jews come together; and in secret spake I nothing. 21 Why askest thou me? ask them that have heard me, what I spake unto them: behold, these know the things which I said. 22 And when he had said this, one of the officers standing by struck Jesus with his hand, saying, Answerest thou the high priest so? 23 Jesus answered him, If I have spoken evil, bear witness of the evil: but if well, why smitest thou me? 24 Annas therefore sent him bound unto Caiaphas the high priest.

25 Now Simon Peter was standing and warming himself. They said therefore unto him, Art thou also one of his disciples? He denied, and said, I am not. 26 One of the servants of the high priest, being a kinsman of him whose ear Peter cut off, saith, Did not I see thee in the garden with him? 27 Peter therefore denied again: and straightway the cock crew.

John has repeatedly asserted that unbelief was due to sin, to moral perversity, to love of evil; the fact could not have been more clearly demonstrated than when Jesus is brought before his enemies for trial. Here the Jewish rulers were really upon trial, and here they condemned themselves.

It is probable that John does not relate the action of the highest ecclesiastical court which is described in the other Gospels. He recounts only a preliminary examination, at the home of the high priest; but the narrative shows the spirit of the judges and the temper of the court which a little later pronounced upon Jesus the sentence of death. It is a revelation of hatred, insincerity, malice, cruelty, and rage. These always characterize the open enemies of Christ. "The high priest . . . asked Jesus of his disciples, and of his teaching," not that he wished information, but only because he desired to entangle Jesus, to extort some word or claim which he could place before the

Sanhedrin as a ground for condemning Jesus.

Jesus replied that his teachings had ever been public and open, and witnesses could testify as to what he had said. There was an implied rebuke of the high priest in the answer of Jesus, and "one of the officers standing by struck Jesus with his hand, saying, Answerest thou the high priest so? Jesus answered him, If I have spoken evil, bear witness of the evil: but if well, why smitest thou me?" They could offer violence to Jesus, but they could not produce witness that his teachings had been false. Just here was their dilemma: they wished to condemn Jesus to death, but they had no proof of guilt or fault, and this has ever been the dilemma of his enemies. Men may hate him and reject him, but they cannot disprove his perfect sinlessness, and in rejecting him they must condemn themselves, as did his enemies of old.

During this examination an incident occurred, in the court of the palace, which was real evidence of the character of Jesus, and which is full of significance for his followers. Peter thrice denied that he knew his Master. He thus showed the divine foresight of the Lord, who only a few hours before had predicted this denial; but he also revealed the weakness of the flesh, and the peril of self-confidence. The disciple who had sworn that he was willing to die for Jesus, and who had rashly drawn a sword in his defense, now blushes and stammers before a few servants, in the dim light of a fire, and declares that he does not belong to the disciples of Jesus. Let us note that it was not his faith that failed, but his courage. He goes out and weeps bitterly. He loves his Lord. He is not a Judas, he will yet be restored, and be commissioned to service in the Master's name.

Before Pilate   Chs. 18:28 to 19:16

While the sentence of death was pronounced by the Jewish court, it could not be executed by Jews. Rome had taken from the subject nation the power of inflicting capital punishment. It was necessary therefore to bring Jesus before the Roman governor to have confirmed the sentence of the Jewish tribunal. In this civil court, as before in the ecclesiastical, his accusers, rather than Jesus, are really on trial; it is not the prisoner but the judge who is finally condemned.

This judge was Pontius Pilate, who, among all the figures of the Gospel narrative, stands out as peculiarly pitiful, weak, and contemptible. Yet he, like Judas, is no monster so far separated from us in depravity as to afford us no warning. You may do today exactly what Pilate did. He is simply an example of a man who lacks decision of character, who does not possess the courage of his convictions, who tries to compromise with wrong, who disobeys conscience through fear of personal loss.

It is not the character and fate of Pilate, however, with which John is especially concerned, but rather with the testimony to Jesus as "the Christ, the Son of God," and with the unbelief of the Jews which, in the presence of Pilate, reaches its incredible climax. This testimony and unbelief are most prominent in the second and the last of the four phases of his civil trial; but the divine character of Jesus and the base craftiness of his enemies are evident in every part of the story.

28 They lead Jesus therefore from Caiaphas into the Prætorium: and it was early; and they themselves entered not into the Prætorium, that they might not be defiled, but might eat the passover. 29 Pilate therefore went out unto them, and saith, What accusation bring ye against this man? 30 They answered and said unto him, If this man were not an evil-doer, we should not have delivered him up unto thee. 31 Pilate therefore said unto them, Take him yourselves, and judge him according to your law. The Jews said unto him, It is not lawful for us to put any man to death: 32 that the word of Jesus might be fulfilled, which he spake, signifying by what manner of death he should die.

(1) First of all the Jews ask Pilate to confirm the death sentence without any process of trial; and this the Roman governor properly refuses to do. How really noble he appears in contrast to the Jewish rulers! How ridiculous, too, is their hypocrisy; they would not enter the palace of the Gentile prince, for fear of ceremonial defilement, but their hearts were black with murderous hate, and they were asking Pilate to condemn an innocent man! How ready we are to "strain out the gnat, and swallow the camel"! They will not go in to Pilate, so he goes out to them, and, through the whole trial, the scene is continually shifting as Pilate speaks first with Jesus within the judgment hall and then with the Jews outside.

Pilate begins by asking what charge they bring against Jesus. (V. 29.) They insolently reply that if he were not a guilty criminal they would not have brought him to be condemned. (V. 30.) The reply of Pilate is clever: "If you have settled the whole matter, if you are the judges, and this is not a case which needs to be tried in a civil court, then proceed to punish the offender according to your power and law, and inflict such punishment as under such conditions is allowable." "Take him yourselves, and judge him according to your law." In this case some minor penalty, but not death, could have been inflicted. The Jews therefore are compelled humbly to admit thât as death is exactly the penalty desired, they will submit the whole case to the civil court. (V. 31.) John notes the significance of this fact. Had Pilate not upheld the Roman law, Jesus would have been stoned; he had predicted for himself the Roman form of execution; his foresight was divine. (V. 32.)

33 Pilate therefore entered again into the Prætorium, and called Jesus, and said unto him, Art thou the King of the Jews? 34 Jesus answered, Sayest thou this of thyself,

*or did others tell it thee concerning me?   35 Pilate an-
swered, Am I a Jew?   Thine own nation and the chief
priests delivered thee unto me: what hast thou done?   36
Jesus answered, My kingdom is not of this world: if my
kingdom were of this world, then would my servants fight,
that I should not be delivered to the Jews: but now is my
kingdom not from hence.   37 Pilate therefore said unto
him, Art thou a king then? Jesus answered, Thou sayest
that I am a king.   To this end have I been born, and to
this end am I come into the world, that I should bear witness unto the truth.   Every one that is of the truth heareth
my voice.   38 Pilate saith unto him, What is truth?*

*And when he had said this, he went out again unto the
Jews, and saith unto them, I find no crime in him.   39 But
ye have a custom, that I should release unto you one at the
passover: will ye therefore that I release unto you the King
of the Jews?   40 They cried out therefore again, saying,
Not this man, but Barabbas.   Now Barabbas was a robber.*

*1 Then Pilate therefore took Jesus, and scourged him.
2 And the soldiers platted a crown of thorns, and put it on
his head, and arrayed him in a purple garment;   3 and
they came unto him, and said, Hail, King of the Jews!
and they struck him with their hands.   4 And Pilate went
out again, and saith unto them, Behold, I bring him out to
you, that ye may know that I find no crime in him.   5
Jesus therefore came out, wearing the crown of thorns and
the purple garment.   And Pilate saith unto them, Behold,
the man!   6 When therefore the chief priests and the officers saw him, they cried out, saying, Crucify him, crucify
him!   Pilate saith unto them, Take him yourselves, and
crucify him: for I find no crime in him.*

(2) As the second stage of the trial opens, the Jews
present their charge; they accuse Jesus of a political crime:
he has called himself a king.   This charge Pilate now in-
vestigates.   "Art thou the King of the Jews?"   The reply of
Jesus constitutes one of the most striking testimonies contained in the Gospel to the fact that "Jesus is the Christ."
Pilate evidently expected a simple negative answer.   The
matter was not so simple as he supposed.   There was a

sense in which Jesus was indeed a king, the true Messiah, the King of Israel; such he claimed to be, such Nathanael had confessed him to be on the first day of his discipleship; in another sense he was not a king, not a political intriguer, not a leader of sedition or rebellion.   He therefore asks Pilate whether the question was intended in a Roman or in a Jewish sense.   (V. 34.)   Pilate replies indignantly: "Am I a Jew?"   He will not tolerate being implicated or interested in Jewish claims and religious subtleties.   He is a Roman judge, and he asks Jesus to tell him plainly what his crime has been.   (V. 35.)   In his reply Jesus reverts to his own question and answers that if Pilate has in mind a political ruler who is attempting to seize power by force of arms, then he is mistaken; but if Pilate is suggesting real influence and authority over the lives and hearts of men, then Jesus is a King.   His instrument is not the sword but the truth; and everyone who loves truth will be his willing subject.   Pilate makes the reply of "frivolous skepticism": "What is truth?"   He sees that whether Jesus is a fanatic or a prophet, he is guilty of no capital crime, and so he determines to release him.   He wishes, however, to secure the favor of the Jews; so he attempts a compromise.   Justice would have granted an immediate acquittal, but self-interest suggests two expedients, both of which fail and lead to the final tragedy.   He first offers to the people, as a special favor, to release Jesus, as the king they had welcomed into the city a few days before, understanding that the plot against Jesus was formed by the Jewish rulers and out of pure envy.   Pilate, however, was disappointed; the rulers persuaded the people to ask for the release of a robber, called Barabbas, and to demand the death of Jesus. (Vs. 38-40.)

Secondly, Pilate gives Jesus over to be scourged.   This was a brutal and inhuman form of torture, as administered by the Romans.   It usually preceded the execution of the death sentence.   Pilate hoped by this to appease the rage of the rulers and to inspire pity in the common people.   To the painful scourging the soldiers added cruel mocking; they crowned the "King" with thorns, they robed him with purple, and showed their homage by smiting him on the face with their hands. Pilate therefore "went out again, and saith unto them, Behold, I bring him out to you, that ye may know that I find no crime in him. Jesus therefore came out, wearing the crown of thorns and the purple garment. And Pilate saith unto them, Behold, the man!" But the expedient failed. The beasts have tasted blood; they howl for more: "Crucify him, crucify him!" (Ch. 19:1-6.)

Pilate is enraged. They are asking him to condemn a man whom he has declared innocent of the charge preferred. "Take him yourselves, and crucify him," he cries; he will himself have no part in such a judicial murder. Nobly spoken! But little did the Roman ruler realize the net the crafty Jews were weaving about him.

7 The Jews answered him, We have a law, and by that law he ought to die, because he made himself the Son of God. 8 When Pilate therefore heard this saying, he was the more afraid; 9 and he entered into the Prætorium again, and saith unto Jesus, Whence art thou? But Jesus gave him no answer. 10 Pilate therefore saith unto him, Speakest thou not unto me? knowest thou not that I have power to release thee, and have power to crucify thee? 11 Jesus answered him, Thou wouldest have no power against me, except it were given thee from above: therefore he that delivered me unto thee hath greater sin.

(3) If Jesus has been found innocent of the one charge, there is another, and they at once accuse Jesus of a religious offense which is truly deserving of death.

"The Jews answered him, We have a law, and by that law he ought to die, because he made himself the Son of God." The Jews were exactly right: Jesus did claim to be the Son of God, and for that claim he deserved to die as a blasphemer, unless he was the Son of God. Here the testi-

mony of John is reaching a climax. Jesus did claim to be
divine; for that claim he was arrested, condemned, crucified. Never for a moment did he deny the charge. He is
either an impostor or divine; there can be no middle
ground.

Upon Pilate the charge has a most unexpected effect:
he is filled with terror. Can anyone today lightly dismiss
the claims of Christ? Even Pilate turns to ask eagerly
whether Jesus has come from above. However ignorant
and superstitious his thoughts, he is intelligent enough to
be arrested by the suggestion that this patient, princely,
innocent sufferer may be a divine Being.

Jesus makes no answer. Why? He never does to a
man who is violating justice, disobeying conscience, and
parleying with sin. It was not the time to ask Jesus as to
his origin, but to declare his innocence and set him free.
Pilate is irritated by the silence of Jesus. He asserts his
dignity: "Speakest thou not unto me? knowest thou not
that I have power to release thee, and have power to
crucify thee?"

Jesus responds in truer dignity: "Thou wouldest have
no power against me, except it were given thee from
above." How solemn the warning: Your power is a divine
trust; beware lest you abuse it. Jesus adds, "Therefore
he that delivered me unto thee hath greater sin," because
he is employing a divinely commissioned officer of the law
as a tool to accomplish his murderous will. What a warning to Caiaphas and his band of guilty conspirators!

*12 Upon this Pilate sought to release him: but the Jews
cried out, saying, If thou release this man, thou art not
Cæsar's friend: every one that maketh himself a king
speaketh against Cæsar. 13 When Pilate therefore heard
these words, he brought Jesus out, and sat down on the
judgment-seat at a place called The Pavement, but in Hebrew, Gabbatha. 14 Now it was the Preparation of the
passover: it was about the sixth hour. And he saith unto
the Jews, Behold, your King! 15 They therefore cried out,*

Away with him, *away with* him, *crucify him!   Pilate saith unto them, Shall I crucify your King?   The chief priests answered, We have no king but Cæsar.   16 Then therefore he delivered him unto them to be crucified.*

(4) Pilate is deeply moved. His one desire now is to release Jesus; but the rulers have one last, desperate resort. They turn upon Pilate with a personal threat: "If thou release this man, thou art not Cæsar's friend." To acquit a Jew who claimed to be a King, how would this sound when reported against Pilate at Rome? The enemy has attacked Pilate in his weakest point; he surrenders on the instant; self-love and self-interest must be regarded at any cost of injustice and crime; his soul is lost. He takes his place upon the judgment seat. He turns to the Jews with the solemn question, spoken in bitter irony: "Shall I crucify your King?" "The chief priests answered, We have no king but Cæsar." Then they are the confessed vassals of Rome, then they have renounced their Messianic hopes, then they have denied their national rights, then they are apostate from God. They have succeeded in accomplishing the death of Jesus, but the success is the failure and the doom of a race. The climax has been reached in the record of Jewish unbelief.

2. THE CRUCIFIXION   Ch. 19:17-42

Before even the briefest survey of the solemn scenes connected with the Passion of our Lord, we should remind ourselves of the significance of the death of Jesus as already stated in this Gospel. According to the testimony of John the Baptist, Jesus was "the Lamb of God, that taketh away the sin of the world," and this removal of guilt involved the death of the sacrifice. Referring to his own death upon the cross, Jesus declared that "as Moses lifted up the serpent in the wilderness, even so must the Son of man be lifted up; . . . that whosoever believeth on him should not perish, but have eternal life." His death therefore was to arrest all the virulent power of sin, in the case of the believer. Jesus further taught that, as "the good shepherd," he was to give his life for the sheep, but in order that they might have life more abundantly. On the last day of his public ministry he asserted that it was the attractive power of his cross which would draw all men unto him. The death of Christ was therefore not merely the voluntary testimony of a martyr to the truth of his teachings; it was an atoning act, removing the guilt and power of sin, drawing men to Christ, and making possible a larger life through faith in him.

As we now turn to the record of the Passion as recorded by John we note that he has completed the narratives of the other Gospels by adding important details; but, what is of far greater importance, we also observe that his account is so framed as to fulfill his supreme purpose of bearing testimony to the Person of Jesus, and of showing the development of faith in him. As the resurrection will demonstrate that Jesus is the Son of God, so this story of the crucifixion will declare him to be the Christ, the Messiah of prophecy.

> *17 They took Jesus therefore: and he went out, bearing the cross for himself, unto the place called The place of a skull, which is called in Hebrew Golgotha: 18 where they crucified him, and with him two others, on either side one, and Jesus in the midst.*

Verses 17-18. In the specific reference to the particular episode of the crucifixion, John spares us all the revolting details of the tragic picture. He simply states that Jesus had to bear his cross, the symbol of infamy and agony; that "they crucified him," and, to identify him more fully with criminals, two others with him, "on either side one, and Jesus in the midst." We need not be told that this form of death was the most shameful and cruel that man had devised; we need only to be reminded that, to secure our salvation, Jesus endured the utmost of disgrace and torture, even the death of the cross.

> *19 And Pilate wrote a title also, and put it on the cross. And there was written, JESUS OF NAZARETH, THE KING OF THE JEWS. 20 This title therefore read many of the Jews, for the place where Jesus was crucified was nigh to the city; and it was written in Hebrew, and in Latin, and in Greek. 21 The chief priests of the Jews therefore said to Pilate, Write not, The King of the Jews; but, that he said, I am King of the Jews. 22 Pilate answered, What I have written I have written.*

Verses 19-22.   It was usual to place an inscription over the head of the cross stating the crime of the sufferer. Pilate, to show his hatred of the rulers, who had really entrapped and defeated him, wrote as a title, "Jesus of Nazareth, the King of the Jews."   He did so in bitter irony; he meant that the only king, or deliverer, the subject Jews could boast or need expect was a helpless sufferer, dying the death of a malefactor.   Pilate, however, like Caiaphas, was affirming more than he intended.   What he stated was the truth, and the very truth John wished to establish by his Gospel, namely, that Jesus was "the Christ," that is, the King of the Jews.   Here, too, was a prophecy: the only Savior of the Jews, their only hope now and ever, is this same crucified Jesus.   Only when they accept him as their King can Israel be saved.

> *23 The soldiers therefore, when they had crucified Jesus, took his garments and made four parts, to every soldier a part; and also the coat: now the coat was without seam, woven from the top throughout. 24 They said therefore one to another, Let us not rend it, but cast lots for it, whose it shall be: that the scripture might be fulfilled, which saith,*
>
> > *They parted my garments among them,*
> > *And upon my vesture did they cast lots.*

Verses 23-24. Of two memorable groups standing near the cross, John first mentions "the soldiers" who "when they had crucified Jesus, took his garments and made four parts, to every soldier a part," and cast lots for his seamless coat. According to law these garments belonged to the executioners. The reference was made not merely to give us a symbol of the callous unbelief in which men can make light of the death of Jesus, or can plan paltry personal gain in the very sight of the cross, but rather to be another proof that "Jesus is the Christ." Even these brutal soldiers were the blind instruments of fulfilling a psalm which had long been interpreted as a prophecy relating to the coming Messiah: "They parted my garments among them, and upon my vesture did they cast lots."

> *25 These things therefore the soldiers did. But there were standing by the cross of Jesus his mother, and his mother's sister, Mary the* wife *of Clopas, and Mary Magdalene. 26 When Jesus therefore saw his mother, and the disciple standing by whom he loved, he saith unto his mother, Woman, behold, thy son! 27 Then saith he to the disciple, Behold, thy mother! And from that hour the disciple took her unto his own* home.

Verses 25-27. Four women seem to have formed the second group, a striking contrast to the four soldiers: the mother of Jesus, his mother's sister, Mary the wife of Clopas, and Mary Magdalene. In connection with the first of these, an incident occurs which as beautifully as any fact in the Gospel history reveals the tender, human sympathy of our Lord. Forgetting his own deep anguish, and mindful only of those he loved, "When Jesus therefore saw his mother, and the disciple standing by whom he loved, he saith unto his mother, Woman, behold, thy son! Then saith he to the disciple, Behold, thy mother! And from that hour the disciple took her unto his own home." In these touching words does John record a supreme example of filial piety, as he shows how Jesus gave to his mother a son, and to his friend a mother.

28 After this Jesus, knowing that all things are now fin-ished, that the scripture might be accomplished, saith, I thirst. 29 There was set there a vessel full of vinegar: so they put a sponge full of the vinegar upon hyssop, and brought it to his mouth. 30 When Jesus therefore had re-ceived the vinegar, he said, It is finished: and he bowed his head, and gave up his spirit.

Verses 28-30. The death of Jesus as recorded by John is described by one suggestive phrase, the meaning of which is imperfectly conveyed by the translation: "He . . . gave up his spirit." The phrase really implies an act which is voluntary and free. No one took his life from him; he had power to lay it down and power to take it again. Therefore when he knew that all things were now accomplished, with kingly majesty, fully conscious of his power, he dismissed his spirit. There are, however, two words, spoken by our Lord, just before his death, the deep significance of which John has noted. The first of these was the cry of the sufferer: "I thirst." It voiced the ut-most experience of physical anguish; but it did more; it exactly fulfilled the inspired prophecy which had foretold the suffering of the Messiah, and, spoken with that proph-ecy in mind, it is recorded as a proof that Jesus is the Christ.

The other word, "It is finished," intimated, as John tells us, a divine consciousness that his earthly mission was ended, that redemption was complete. For those who are burdened by the guilt of sin, nothing remains to be done but to accept him as the Lamb of God; for those who have been stricken by the power of sin, there is eternal life if they look in trust to the uplifted Christ. Such is the issue of faith in the divine Son of God.

31 The Jews therefore, because it was the Preparation, that the bodies should not remain on the cross upon the sabbath (for the day of that sabbath was a high day), asked of Pilate that their legs might be broken, and that they might be taken away. 32 The soldiers therefore came,

and brake the legs of the first, and of the other that was
crucified with him: 33 but when they came to Jesus, and
saw that he was dead already, they brake not his legs: 34
howbeit one of the soldiers with a spear pierced his side,
and straightway there came out blood and water. 35 And
he that hath seen hath borne witness, and his witness is
true: and he knoweth that he saith true, that ye also may
believe. 36 For these things came to pass, that the scrip-
ture might be fulfilled, A bone of him shall not be broken.
37 And again another scripture saith, They shall look on
him whom they pierced.

Verses 31-37. While the body of Jesus still hung upon
the cross, an incident occurred which occasioned the fulfillment of two further prophecies and is interpreted by
John as a double proof that Jesus is the Christ. According to Jewish law it was necessary to remove from sight,
before sunset, the bodies of executed criminals. The enemies of Jesus were the more eager to obey this law because
of the sacred character of the day which was to begin. In
order to hasten the death of the three sufferers, permission
was received from Pilate to have their legs broken. "But
when they came to Jesus, and saw that he was dead already, they brake not his legs: howbeit one of the soldiers
with a spear pierced his side, and straightway there came
out blood and water." The nature and meaning of the
blood and water are difficult to determine. John interprets
them in his First Epistle as symbols of redemption and
evidences of divine incarnation; but here the thought is
fixed on the proof from fulfilled prophecy that Jesus is the
Christ. It had been provided, in reference to the paschal
lamb: "A bone of him shall not be broken"; this was now
true in the offering up of "the Lamb of God"; and Zech-
ariah had referred to the coming of the Messiah in the
words, "They shall look on him whom they pierced."
There was evidence then, in the pierced side, that Jesus
was the Christ. A larger fulfillment of the latter prophecy
remains for the future; someday Israel in awe and sor-

row and repentance will "look on him whom they pierced," as he reappears in heavenly majesty, and then will begin the true glory of the converted and believing nation.

> *38 And after these things Joseph of Arimathæa, being a disciple of Jesus, but secretly for fear of the Jews, asked of Pilate that he might take away the body of Jesus: and Pilate gave* him *leave. He came therefore, and took away his body. 39 And there came also Nicodemus, he who at the first came to him by night, bringing a mixture of myrrh and aloes, about a hundred pounds. 40 So they took the body of Jesus, and bound it in linen cloths with the spices, as the custom of the Jews is to bury. 41 Now in the place where he was crucified there was a garden; and in the garden a new tomb wherein was never man yet laid. 42 There then because of the Jews' Preparation (for the tomb was nigh at hand) they laid Jesus.*

Verses 38-42.   The burial of Jesus presents a picture of pathetic and melancholy interest.   Two men, who had lacked the courage of their convictions and had failed to give their support and encouragement to Jesus while he was living, now come forward to pay him honor after he is dead.   These are both rulers, men of position and power, Joseph of Arimathea, and Nicodemus; the former lays the body of Jesus in his own new tomb, the second wraps the body in a profusion of rich spices.   These may have been deeds of courage and of love, but they came too late; not too late to fulfill prophecy, nor to render a real service to the cause of Christ, but too late, surely, to afford satisfaction to the hearts of the two men who mourned their cowardice and remembered with poignant regret what they might have been and might have done.   Their faith is like a glow of sunset at the close of the dark day of cruel and murderous unbelief; but as we turn from its shadows let us remember that Jesus does not ask for secret disciples; he bore the painful cross for us, and he expects us openly, courageously, willingly, to take up the cross and follow him.

3. THE RESURRECTION Ch. 20

Now the night has gone; the bright dawn has burst; Jesus has risen from the dead! With the same physical body which Joseph had placed in his rock-hewn sepulcher, bearing the marks of the spear thrust and the nails, Jesus has appeared to his disciples; and, as unbelief found its consummation in his cross, so faith reaches its climax at the sight of the empty tomb, and in the vision of a risen Lord.

As we review the four scenes painted by John, we should notice the nature of the evidence to the fact of the resurrection which each presents, secondly, the content of the faith inspired, and thirdly, the prophecy which each contains of the life in which faith will issue.

1 Now on the first day of the week cometh Mary Magdalene early, while it was yet dark, unto the tomb, and seeth the stone taken away from the tomb. 2 She runneth therefore, and cometh to Simon Peter, and to the other disciple whom Jesus loved, and saith unto them, They have taken away the Lord out of the tomb, and we know not where they have laid him. 3 Peter therefore went forth, and the other disciple, and they went toward the tomb. 4 And they ran both together: and the other disciple outran Peter, and came first to the tomb; 5 and stooping and looking in, he seeth the linen cloths lying; yet entered he not in. 6 Simon Peter therefore also cometh, following him, and entered into the tomb; and he beholdeth the linen cloths lying, 7 and the napkin, that was upon his head, not lying with the linen cloths, but rolled up in a place by itself. 8 Then entered in therefore the other disciple also, who came first to the tomb, and he saw, and believed. 9 For as yet they knew not the scripture, that he must rise again from the dead. 10 So the disciples went away again unto their own home.

Verses 1-10. This first scene depicts Peter and John at the tomb of Jesus early on the morning of the resurrec-

tion. They do not know that Jesus has risen; they are not
expecting him to rise. They have been summoned by the
announcement of Mary Magdalene: "They have taken
away the Lord out of the tomb, and we know not where
they have laid him." They have run to the tomb, and
have found it empty. Peter now turns away bewildered
and distressed; but when he sees the tomb empty, and the
cloths which had been about the body of Jesus undis-
turbed, and the napkin which had been about his head
carefully "rolled up in a place by itself," John believes.
He concludes that there is only one explanation of the facts
before him: Jesus has risen from the dead. There is no
other explanation of the empty tomb, but men have been
suggesting others ever since: " 'His disciples came by night,
and stole him away' "; "Jesus did not really die, he only
swooned upon the cross, and then revived and escaped
from the tomb"; "the disciples never saw him, they only
imagined that he rose"; "his followers were guilty of in-
tentional falsehood." These answers to the problem have
been attempted: theft, resuscitation, hallucination, deception; there is only one answer for the thoughtful mind:
resurrection.

What was it, however, that John believed? That Jesus
had risen? Surely this, but further that, as he had risen,
he was therefore the divine Son of God. The conviction
then produced was the origin of this Gospel, the source
of a life of loving devotion for the apostle John. Such,
too, in the mind of the writer, is the only possible conclusion to draw from the fact of the resurrection; Jesus must
be divine, and deserving of our devotion and our love.

*11 But Mary was standing without at the tomb weeping:
so, as she wept, she stooped and looked into the tomb; 12
and she beholdeth two angels in white sitting, one at the
head, and one at the feet, where the body of Jesus had
lain. 13 And they say unto her, Woman, why weepest
thou? She saith unto them, Because they have taken away
my Lord, and I know not where they have laid him. 14*

*When she had thus said, she turned herself back, and be-
holdeth Jesus standing, and knew not that it was Jesus. 15
Jesus saith unto her, Woman, why weepest thou? whom
seekest thou? She, supposing him to be the gardener, saith
unto him, Sir, if thou hast borne him hence, tell me where
thou hast laid him, and I will take him away. 16 Jesus
saith unto her, Mary. She turneth herself, and saith unto
him in Hebrew, Rabboni; which is to say, Teacher. 17
Jesus saith to her, Touch me not; for I am not yet ascended
unto the Father: but go unto my brethren, and say to them,
I ascend unto my Father and your Father, and my God
and your God. 18 Mary Magdalene cometh and telleth
the disciples, I have seen the Lord; and that he had said
these things unto her.*

Verses 11-18. Mary Magdalene was the first person
to whom the risen Lord appeared. She had come to the
tomb to weep, and to pay homage to the body of the
dead; she was surprised by a vision of angels, and was
convinced of the resurrection by a single spoken word.
She saw Jesus but did not recognize him until her own
name fell from his lips: "Mary. She turneth herself, and
saith unto him in Hebrew, Rabboni; which is to say,
Teacher." It is the mourner who stands weeping at the
grave of buried hopes who, perhaps first of all, needs
the vision of a risen Christ; and sometimes he speaks, to
the very heart, a message which inspires as true a faith as
that which comes to John as he reasons from the fact of
an empty tomb.

What is the message to Mary; what the content of her
faith? That Jesus is a divine Being, who stands in an
absolutely unique relation to the Father, as the Son of
God. Jesus bids her tell the disciples that he is about to
ascend, not to our Father, but "unto my Father and your
Father, and my God and your God."

What further was the life which was to issue from belief in him, and as a result of his ascension? A fellowship with himself, more intimate and real than his fol-

lowers had ever known, a fellowship made possible by the gift of the Spirit. Therefore Jesus designates his disciples by a name he had never used before: "My brethren." This also explains the words of Jesus, "Touch me not; for I am not yet ascended." It was not yet the time, even for reverent love, and even by a symbolic touch, to claim the fellowship which death had broken or the true communion which his ascension was to secure. "Not yet"; but now that he has come to dwell with believers as an abiding spiritual presence, now we have the truest fellowship "with the Father, and with his Son Jesus Christ."

> *19 When therefore it was evening, on that day, the first day of the week, and when the doors were shut where the disciples were, for fear of the Jews, Jesus came and stood in the midst, and saith unto them, Peace be unto you. 20 And when he had said this, he showed unto them his hands and his side. The disciples therefore were glad, when they saw the Lord. 21 Jesus therefore said to them again, Peace be unto you: as the Father hath sent me, even so send I you. 22 And when he had said this, he breathed on them, and saith unto them, Receive ye the Holy Spirit: 23 whose soever sins ye forgive, they are forgiven unto them; whose soever sins ye retain, they are retained.*

Verses 19-23. The first appearance to the disciples occurred the same day, in the evening, when, fearing the Jews, they had withdrawn for safety to an upper room. They believed the fact of the resurrection, not when reported to them by credible witnesses, but on the evidence of a physical demonstration: "Jesus . . . stood in the midst. . . . And . . . he showed unto them his hands and his side." Such proof was needed then, but not now. Other kinds of evidence should suffice for us. We should know the blessedness of those who "have not seen, and yet have believed." Their faith was now in one who was unquestionably divine, one who could give peace to the soul, one who could impart the Spirit of God, one who was indeed the Son of God. The life on which they were to enter, as his followers, was to be, in its essence, a great mission, identical with the mission of the divine Son. His mission had not ended, it would not end: "As the Father hath sent me [a perfect tense], even so send I you [a present tense]." The disciples were to carry on the work of the Master. The power, too, was to be his: "He breathed on them, and saith unto them, Receive ye the Holy Spirit." This gift imparted to them a fuller knowledge of the truth; it was completed in the greater gift at Pentecost. The Spirit, through the agency of those who testified for Christ, was to secure the pardon of believers and the condemnation of unbelief. Thus the risen Christ was to carry on his saving work through his human messengers, by the power of his divine Spirit.

24 But Thomas, one of the twelve, called Didymus, was not with them when Jesus came. 25 The other disciples therefore said unto him, We have seen the Lord. But he said unto them, Except I shall see in his hands the print of the nails, and put my finger into the print of the nails, and put my hand into his side, I will not believe.

26 And after eight days again his disciples were within, and Thomas with them. Jesus cometh, the doors being shut, and stood in the midst, and said, Peace be unto you. 27 Then saith he to Thomas, Reach hither thy finger, and see my hands; and reach hither thy hand, and put it into my side: and be not faithless, but believing. 28 Thomas answered and said unto him, My Lord and my God. 29 Jesus saith unto him, Because thou hast seen me, thou hast believed: blessed are they that have not seen, and yet have believed.

Verses 24-29. In his second appearance to the disciples, one week later, the purpose of Jesus was to convince Thomas of the reality of his resurrection. This disciple has been known commonly as "the doubter." In a sense, he was no more skeptical than the others had been, before they had seen the risen Christ. When he heard their report, he demanded practically the same proof that had been given them. He should, however, have accepted their testimony. It was his fault, and it is of the very essence of doubt, to demand a peculiar and specific kind of proof, and to refuse to believe on other and sufficient ground. That he was an "honest doubter" is certain, (1) because of his attitude toward the evidence. He went to the meeting of the disciples, to the very place where he would hear repeated the testimony he regarded as inadequate. (2) He was not afraid of the consequences of belief. He loved the Master and had been willing to die with him. When one is willing to face the evidence, and really loves Christ, he is certain to receive light.

Conviction came to Thomas as the Lord appeared and offered to give the kind of evidence desired. Then Thomas believed, but without demanding the proof he had before required. He was convinced by the love and mercy and knowledge of his Lord, not only of his resurrection, but of his divine nature. He cried out in adoring wonder: "My Lord and my God." This confession is not only the culmination of belief; it is also the climax of the Gospel. John at once adds that his purpose in writing has been to bring his readers to just such faith in Christ. If one naturally so skeptical as Thomas was convinced that Jesus rose from the dead, we have no excuse for doubt. If Jesus did so rise, then we should argue, as did Thomas, that he is divine. If Jesus allowed Thomas to worship him as God, we should yield ourselves to him in adoration and love as to a divine Master, who has been proved to be, by his resurrection from the dead, "very God, of very God."

THE CONCLUSION

30 Many other signs therefore did Jesus in the presence of the disciples, which are not written in this book: 31 but these are written, that ye may believe that Jesus is the Christ, the Son of God; and that believing ye may have life in his name.

In these words John states both his method and purpose in writing this Gospel. He has not intended to compose a life of Jesus. His aim has been to select from a vast array of facts only a sufficient number to convince the readers that "Jesus is the Christ, the Son of God." By the first term, "the Christ," he designates the office of the Messiah, in whom were fulfilled all the prophecies concerning the Redeemer and Savior of the world; by the term "Son of God," he denotes the divine Person of our Lord. The proof presented is that of "signs"; by these John means not only those of this chapter, but the miracles related in his entire narrative. Among these "signs" the resurrection of Jesus is supreme; when it has been accepted by Thomas he at once believes, and confesses his faith. To produce such faith in others is the purpose of the writer. He addresses, however, not chiefly those who are unbelieving, but evidently those who already have faith in Christ. He has given us a narrative in which we have seen how faith can be increased and developed, and he here intimates that a like experience of enlarging belief will be ours, if we carefully study these "signs" wrought by our divine Lord. Most of all he encourages his readers by the statement that his aim is practical not speculative, moral not intellectual; he wishes them to believe in order that they may have life; he assures them that creed will affect character, that belief will result in experience, that faith will determine conduct. John has written this Gospel in order that we may know Christ, may trust him, may commit ourselves to him, and thus have life in all its fullness of peace and joy and beauty and fruitfulness and hope, even the life eternal which issues from a knowledge of the true God revealed in Jesus Christ his Son.

IV

THE EPILOGUE.
THE PRESENCE AND THE
SYMBOLIC "SIGN"

Ch. 21

This charming scene, in which the risen Christ meets his disciples by the inland lake, is regarded as an addition, or an appendix, to the Gospel. It is vitally related, however, to the great truths of the book, and is in perfect harmony with its contents. Before this chapter opens, the argument of the writer has been concluded; but by it his message is enforced and enlarged, and an artistic literary completeness is given to his work.

Here a symbolic "sign" and a specific prophecy attest the divine nature of Christ; here the essence of faith is set forth as loving obedience; here life is interpreted in terms of service.

At the bidding of their Master, the disciples had returned to Galilee, where he had promised they should see him. While they waited for him to appear, a group of seven returned to their former task as fishermen. After a long night of unsuccessful toil, in the early dawn, they saw Jesus standing on the shore; but they did not recognize him. At his suggestion they again let down their net, and were surprised by a miraculous catch of fish. John at once discerned the presence and act of the divine Lord; Peter hastened to swim ashore, in his eagerness to greet the Master; the others followed in the boat, and "when they got out upon the land, they see a fire of coals there, and fish laid thereon, and bread. . . . And none of the disciples durst inquire of him, Who art thou? knowing that it was the Lord." By this unexpected appearance, as by each similar manifestation after his resurrection, Jesus was making it more easy for his disciples to believe what he had told them of a time soon to come, when, by his Spirit, he would be with them continually. The first message of this chapter, therefore, is that of the personal presence of Christ with all believers. Sometimes, after long hours of lonely toil, or in the dark night of weariness, we remember the Savior's promise, and realize his presence and find peace and gladness and hope, as we greet the dawn of a brighter day. The essential message of this closing scene of the Gospel relates, however, to Christian service.

1 After these things Jesus manifested himself again to the disciples at the sea of Tiberias; and he manifested him-self on this wise. 2 There were together Simon Peter, and Thomas called Didymus, and Nathanael of Cana in Galilee, and the sons of Zebedee, and two other of his disciples. 3 Simon Peter saith unto them, I go a fishing. They say unto him, We also come with thee. They went forth, and entered into the boat; and that night they took nothing. 4 But when day was now breaking, Jesus stood on the beach: yet the disciples knew not that it was Jesus. 5 Jesus therefore saith unto them, Children, have ye aught to eat? They answered him, No. 6 And he said unto them, Cast the net on the right side of the boat, and ye shall find. They cast therefore, and now they were not able to draw it for the multitude of fishes. 7 That disciple therefore whom Jesus loved saith unto Peter, It is the Lord. So when Simon Peter heard that it was the Lord, he girt his coat about him (for he was naked), and cast himself into the sea. 8 But the other disciples came in the little boat (for they were not far from the land, but about two hun-dred cubits off), dragging the net full of fishes. 9 So when they got out upon the land, they see a fire of coals there, and fish laid thereon, and bread. 10 Jesus saith unto them, Bring of the fish which ye have now taken. 11 Simon Peter therefore went up, and drew the net to land, full of

*great fishes, a hundred and fifty and three: and for all there
were so many, the net was not rent. 12 Jesus saith unto
them, Come and break your fast. And none of the disciples durst inquire of him, Who art thou? knowing that it
was the Lord. 13 Jesus cometh, and taketh the bread, and
giveth them, and the fish likewise. 14 This is now the third
time that Jesus was manifested to the disciples, after that
he was risen from the dead.*

Verses 1-14. The "sign" of the miraculous draught of
fishes is not to be confused with a similar miracle wrought
by our Lord at the opening of his ministry; it is, however,
to be interpreted in the light of that previous event. On
that former occasion Jesus stated clearly the truth he
wished to illustrate: "Come ye after me, and I will make
you fishers of men." So now it required no word of explanation to impress upon his disciples the truth that he
had called them to undertake for him the work of "saving
men alive." This was to be the character of their service.
In this task of winning souls for Christ, every Christian is
concerned. Opportunities and talents differ: but it is the
privilege and duty of all to be "fishers of men."

So, too, the "sign" suggests the guidance which the Master is ever ready to give, and upon which we must depend
in case our service is to be successful. These men toiled
all the night and took nothing: but Jesus "said unto them,
Cast the net on the right side of the boat, and ye shall find.
They cast therefore, and now they were not able to draw
it for the multitude of fishes." How often we stand in need
of some directing word from our Master!

The "sign" declares further that we can depend upon
the power of our Lord in doing his work. The miracle is
not to be explained on the ground, merely, that Jesus knew
the best place to fish; but rather that all things were subject to him, including, as the psalmist suggests, "the fish
of the sea, whatsoever passeth through the paths of the
seas." As we undertake the service of the Master, we
should be encouraged by the belief that he has all power
"in heaven and on earth."

Then again the story tells us of the support which the Master gives his servants. We can depend not only upon his power to do the work but upon his grace to give what we are needing for the body and the soul. When the disciples come to land they find the broiled fish and the bread ready for their morning meal, and to this provision they are told to add from the abundant supply in the net. The latter is described as containing "a hundred and fifty and three" great fish; so there was provision for the future as well as for the present. As servants of Christ we are to receive "of his fulness," "and grace for grace."

15 So when they had broken their fast, Jesus saith to Simon Peter, Simon, son of John, lovest thou me more than these? He saith unto him, Yea, Lord; thou knowest that I love thee. He saith unto him, Feed my lambs. 16 He saith to him again a second time, Simon, son of John, lovest thou me? He saith unto him, Yea, Lord; thou knowest that I love thee. He saith unto him, Tend my sheep. 17 He saith unto him the third time, Simon, son of John, lovest thou me? Peter was grieved because he said unto him the third time, Lovest thou me? And he said unto him, Lord, thou knowest all things; thou knowest that I love thee. Jesus saith unto him, Feed my sheep. 18 Verily, verily, I say unto thee, When thou wast young, thou girdedst thyself, and walkedst whither thou wouldest: but when thou shalt be old, thou shalt stretch forth thy hands, and another shall gird thee, and carry thee whither thou wouldest not. 19 Now this he spake, signifying by what manner of death he should glorify God. And when he had spoken this, he saith unto him, Follow me. 20 Peter, turning about, seeth the disciple whom Jesus loved following; who also leaned back on his breast at the supper, and said, Lord, who is he that betrayeth thee? 21 Peter therefore seeing him saith to Jesus, Lord, and what shall this man do? 22 Jesus saith unto him, If I will that he tarry till I come, what is that to thee? follow thou me. 23 This saying therefore went forth among the brethren, that that disciple should not die: yet Jesus said not unto him, that he should not die; but, If I will that he tarry till I come, what is that to thee?

Verses 15-23. In the dialogue between our Lord and Peter there is further instruction as to the nature of service. Here the apostle is given by the Master a threefold commission: "Feed my lambs"; "Tend my sheep"; "Feed my sheep." It is necessary to "save men alive" by casting the Gospel net, and bringing men to Christ in living faith; but it is also necessary to guide believers in the way of truth, to shepherd them with pastoral care, and to feed them with the Word of life. This work is assigned in more special measure to some Christians than to others, yet there is none who cannot have a part in this blessed ministry.

The more specific message, in connection with this commission of Peter is, however, for all believers alike. It concerns not so much the form as the condition, or motive, of service. This is declared to be love for Christ. Peter had denied his Lord, and forfeited his place as an apostle; Jesus, after his resurrection, had met with Peter alone, and undoubtedly had given pardon to the penitent disciple; but now he is publicly to reinstate him in office, and before so doing he draws from Peter a declaration of his devoted love. Three different questions are asked, three replies given, and each is followed by the welcome command to public, apostolic service. Jesus is undoubtedly calling to mind the threefold denial of Peter, and also the proud boast of surpassing love which had preceded it. "Simon, son of John, lovest thou me more than these?" asks the Master, referring to the self-confident promise of Peter to follow the Master even though all the other apostles should fail.

In his reply Peter does affirm his love, but humbled by the memory of his fall, he uses a less emphatic word than that of his Master: "Yea, Lord; thou knowest that I love thee." He does not claim a perfect, complete devotion; he feels that his denial disproves such love; but looking into his own heart he cannot deny a supreme admiration, a true affection for his Lord. Jesus saith unto him: "Feed my lambs."

Jesus now alters his question; he omits the phrase which had rebuked the former boast of Peter: "Lovest thou me?" Peter replies as before, using for "love" a humbler term than the Master, and again appealing to the testimony of the Master's own knowledge of Peter's heart, as he affirms his affection: "Yea, Lord; thou knowest that I love thee." Jesus saith unto him: "Tend my sheep."

Again Jesus changes the form of his question; this time he substitutes the term for "love" that Peter had used, and seems to ask whether Peter really had even such humble and imperfect devotion as he was claiming. Peter is deeply grieved, not only by the repetition of the question, but also by this change in its form. He cannot deny his own consciousness, however, even though he once did deny his Lord; he knows that he loves the Master, and cannot but affirm that love, and he now appeals for confirmation to the inmost, divine knowledge of Christ which he emphasizes by an added phrase: "Lord, thou knowest all things; thou knowest that I love thee." Yes, the Lord does know; and for this reason he repeats a third time his inspiring commission: "Feed my sheep." We, too, may have denied our Master, by word or deed; but if we have truly repented, and if in our hearts there is a sincere love for Christ we need not hesitate, in humble dependence upon him, to enter anew even public service in his cause.

In the case of Peter, and in the experience of all the servants of Christ, there will be opportunities of expressing love more forcibly than by the utterance of words however carefully selected. Suffering is usually the accompaniment of service, and the test of love. Peter was to prove his devotion to Christ by a martyr's death; and of this fact he is now tenderly informed by his Master, who then bids Peter to follow him. Looking behind him, Peter sees his dear friend, John, following with them, and at once asks what his experience is to be. Jesus replies: "If I will that he tarry till I come, what is that to thee? follow thou me." Of course Jesus did not intend to suggest that we are not to take a deep interest in the fate of others, but he wishes us to be kept from all envy and discontent which comparisons may produce; and he desires us to be concerned, rather, as to our absolute fidelity to him. He is specially suggesting a lesson in the time of service. For one, the allotted season is brief, the pangs of death severe, the heavenly rest near at hand; for another there are long years of testimony, and of waiting for the Lord's return. "This saying therefore went forth among the brethren, that that disciple should not die: yet Jesus said not unto him, that he should not die; but, If I will that he tarry till I come, what is that to thee?" The coming of Christ, therefore, does not refer to death, but to his return in glory, when the dead shall be raised and living believers transformed, and together "caught up . . . to meet the Lord in the air" that they ever may "be with the Lord." This has been the blessed hope of every generation of Christians, and it should encourage us to such fidelity in service that we ever can pray, "Come, Lord Jesus."

24 This is the disciple that beareth witness of these things, and wrote these things: and we know that his witness is true.

25 And there are also many other things which Jesus did, the which if they should be written every one, I suppose that even the world itself would not contain the books that should be written.

Verses 24-25. Two brief words close this Epilogue. The first affirms the truthfulness and credibility of John as a witness to the facts which the Gospel relates. The more carefully one reads this remarkable book the more ardently will he assent to this testimony. The author must have been not only an eyewitness, and a man of the most profound spiritual vision, but one who in special measure received the aid of the Spirit who has promised to guide the disciples of Christ into all truth.

The last verse, in pardonable hyperbole, asserts that

"there are also many other things which Jesus did, the which if they should be written every one, I suppose that even the world itself would not contain the books that should be written." The meaning evidently is this: that no writings, however true, could comprehend the infinite glory manifested by the divine Son of God. Of that glory this Gospel affords us a glimpse, but it is so satisfying, so splendid, so alluring, that we love to linger in its light, and we yearn for that clearer vision when we shall meet him face-to-face and "shall be like him" when we "see him even as he is."